GROW
YOUR
WINGS

JAKOB GALLAGHER

Dedication

I write this book and dedicate it to my family—those who came before me and those to come after. My Grandpa Dave Gallagher once told me, before he passed away, that he wished he had written a book about his life. I certainly wish he did, too. Just as I peeked him into this story and was able to tell you a little bit about him, I sure hope he is peeking down from heaven and smiling at this book. I dedicate this to you, papa. I secondly dedicate this to my children. Many of you aren't here yet, but you soon will be. Look upon the mighty hand of the Lord and see His faithfulness.

The testimony of Jesus is the spirit of prophecy. That means what He has done in me, I declare He will do the same and even greater in you. The Lord has already spoken to me on your behalf, my sons and daughter. Please listen to me … Bookmark this page! You will be far greater than I am and go further than your mother or I ever could imagine. I already know it. How do we know, you may ask? Because we've prayed that you would before you were even on this earth. He is going to ask you to do some unimaginable things in your life, and you will need to refer back to this book for the courage to grow your wings. Read this to remember His faithfulness in me so that you will know His faithfulness will continue in you. Take courage; times will look scary in your lifetime, but remember He who is in you is greater than he who is in the world. I love you. I dedicate this also to my parents, my beloved warrior of a mother, and my best friend of a father. I would never be where I am without your love and guidance. Finally, I saved the best for last; I dedicate this book to my radiant wife. Rebekah Gallagher, you have changed my life in more ways than one, and I pray you know just how deeply I love you every single day that we get to share together here on earth. Our legacy will shine for His glory.

Forewords

Jeff Rostocil (Author of Unshakable)

Crazy.

We use the word crazy to describe a lunatic or an unpredictable experience. Someone crazy is insane. Something crazy is outrageous. There is, however, a dictionary definition of crazy that describes passion. In this sense, crazy simply is being possessed by enthusiasm and excitement.

All the heroes of the Bible were a bit crazy in that they possessed enthusiasm for God and His purposes. Their passion subdued kingdoms, obtained promises, stopped the mouths of lions, escaped the edge of the sword, made them valiant in battle, and raised the dead. It should not surprise us that the most influential Christian writer in history was also accused of being out of his mind (Acts 26:24-25).

Paul the Apostle certainly lived a crazy life. He saw the resurrected Jesus in all His glory. He challenged emperors, performed miracles, raised the dead, penned two-thirds of the most prolific ancient document, and sojourned to unreached nations, making the Gospel available to the entire Western world.

Yet, his enthusiasm did not exempt him from facing hardship. We read of Paul being beaten, imprisoned, whipped, shipwrecked, deprived of food, bitten by snakes, betrayed by friends, blinded for three days, rejected by his countrymen, stoned to death, and unceremoniously martyred at the hands of a deranged king.

What Paul's life teaches us is that before we can ever find crazy success, we must overcome challenges, sometimes impossible challenges. Abraham was childless. Joseph was a slave. Moses was abandoned at birth. David was a fugitive. Hannah was barren. Elijah hid in a cave. Daniel was sentenced to death. Mary was pregnant out of wedlock.

In this book, you will read about one man's insane faith, one couple's outrageous courage, and one family's outlandish obedience. Jakob Gallagher's journey will inspire you, uplift you, and hopefully catapult you into your own crazy adventures with the Holy Spirit. Like yours, his journey is unique. Yet, his story is no different from the rest of us.

Jakob Gallagher's life did not play out the way he envisioned. Life seldom does. But this man trusted in God, leaned on His promises, and overcame the obstacles. This is the heritage of the godly, for we are more than overcomers through Christ who loves us (Rom. 8:37).

You have struggles? Good. You have obstacles? Perfect. This book reminds us that our obstacles are our opportunities for greatness. Let us not forget that being more than an overcomer implies that we will have something to overcome. After all, only through perseverance did the snail reach the ark!

Like all that have gone before us, our road to success requires perseverance. Count on your path being riddled with failure, setbacks, and disappointments. But you can learn from the snail and take up the faith of your forefathers. Their victory is your opportunity to rise.

It's been said that the journey of a lifetime starts with turning a page. This book in your hand can be the start of your new journey. As you turn the pages of this book, let God turn the pages of your heart. Leave behind that which has no life in it and embrace all that is eternal.

In the spiritual and cultural battle for truth, you could lose everything. You could lose your possessions. It could cost you your reputation, your loved ones, and maybe even your own life. But there is one thing your enemy can never take from you - your testimony.

Jakob has poured out his heart for you in these words. His passion permeates these pages with the presence of God. His story is Heaven's testimony to you. May it encourage you to make your move and grow your wings.

Matthew Gonzales

From the moment I first met Jakob Gallagher, I knew there was something extraordinary about him. Watching him grow up and become the man he is today—a true world-changer—has been one of the greatest privileges of my life. His story is not just a recounting of personal events but a bold invitation to witness the hand of God weaving a masterpiece through the unknown, the trials, and the triumphs.

Now, in Grow Your Wings, Jakob invites us into his remarkable journey, offering us a front-row seat to the power of a life fully surrendered to God. Our personal stories hold incredible power. First, they remind us of the unique ways God moves through each of our lives, using even our challenges to shape us for His purpose. Second, they inspire others to find hope, faith, and courage for their own journeys. As Jakob shares his own story, he reminds us that every life has the potential to create a ripple effect of faith and transformation. As C.S. Lewis so aptly put it, "You can't go back and change the beginning, but you can start where you are and change the ending."

Jakob's journey is nothing short of inspiring. It is a testament to the power of faith, the transformative nature of surrender, and the beauty of trusting a God who still performs miracles. His experiences are not just his own; they resonate deeply with the universal longing for purpose, hope, and an enduring legacy. Jakob doesn't simply tell his story—he invites you to step into it, to see yourself in its pages, and to encounter the God who makes the impossible possible.

What sets this book apart is not just the authenticity with which Jakob shares his highs and lows but the way his narrative points us beyond ourselves—to the God who faithfully leads us through the unknown. Jakob's story is a declaration that no matter how uncertain life may seem, God is always present, always working, and always faithful.

As you turn these pages, prepare to be challenged, uplifted, and inspired. This is more than an autobiography; it's a journey of faith that will encourage you to embrace your own story and trust the Author of it all. Jakob Gallagher has lived a life that reminds us all that our stories, when surrendered to God, can birth legacies far beyond what we can imagine.

Zee Sav

GROW YOUR WINGS by Jakob Gallagher is an adventure you want to join as soon as you begin reading. Through all of the ups and downs of Jakob and Rebekah's journey, you'll find yourself reading with such joy! That's God's anointing. What a remarkable book. I'm sure it will rock your world as it did mine."

Joe Poni (Author of *Follow Your Curiosity*)

Jake shares a firsthand journey, illustrating his experience of trusting the Lord at every step from youth to maturity. You can't help but feel inspired and challenged with each chapter. *Grow Your Wings* has the power to kindle a personal awakening in faith and a deep reliance on God.

Mildred Hooper

Grow Your Wings is a riveting story of courage, tenacity, and pressing on against all odds while wholeheartedly trusting God with the outcome amid difficult decisions. It's an inspiring story of growing into your own identity and releasing the plans and details of your ENTIRE LIFE, FAMILY, AND FUTURE into the hands of a sovereign, loving, almighty God and believing that HE ORCHESTRATES the steps of the righteous.

I cried SEVERAL times as I saw the hand of God in Jake's and Rebekah's lives. I have personally seen the faithfulness of God and HIS promises for them being fulfilled in their lives through their obedience.

It is an inspiring story that EVERYONE who has ever questioned the faithfulness of God and if He still answers prayer needs to read.

Who Am I Writing This to?

From Jakob Gallagher

I'm writing this to the generations of the generations that I may not ever see, but in my day and age, I am declaring that you will surely taste the fruit of your forefather and foremother, Jakob and Rebekah Gallagher—a message to our children; to our children and our children's children. There were many great and renowned people who came before you and blazed trails that were so beautiful. There are countless names to mention. Above all, this is dedicated to telling you to remember that you are never alone, to remind you that the Lord has never forsaken you, and to assure you that you are loved, cared for, and thought about. Even if we are never able to physically lay our eyes upon you or, with our voice, tell you how much we love you, this we know is certain.

Let it be known that our God is the God of the generations. Our God is the God of inheritance. Our God is the God of legacy, and He is still the God of Abraham, Isaac, and Jacob even to this day. Even though Rebekah and I were once strangers in the land that we had never known, you are now standing in a place and in a promise to take dominion, fill your quivers, and expand territory. Let love abound in your hearts, let peace wash over your minds, let the truth of the Lord be your buckler, and remember that in your day of trouble, call upon the name of the Lord, and He **WILL** answer you (Psalms 50:15).

My Current Situation

Today is March 20th of the year 2022, and I will be 26 years old in July. I just started writing this today. About a year ago, I and my beloved wife, Rebekah, said farewell to the only life we had ever known—25 years in California. We were the wild ones. We were crazy enough to follow this constantly knocking desire on the door of our hearts, ultimately leading us to move to the land of Texas—a land we knew nothing of and have never been to. The book will highlight in more detail about how God got us here and how we learned to "Grow Our Wings" along the way. We moved here for several reasons, but none more than for our children's heritage, our legacy, and our future babies on our minds. Although we didn't know, God said, "go."

Crazily enough, when we arrived here about eight months later, I was told that the possibility of us having biological children was nearly IMPOSSIBLE. It broke me. However, today, I sit here on a couch writing to you (my children) in faith, where Rebekah and I have just purchased a house in a small town in Texas as a prophetic declaration that our Faithful God would fill every room. Rebekah and I's greatest desire is to be your parents and see you serve the Lord. No job, no fame, no amount of money could ever compare to the value you carry in our sight. We pray for you every single night, and we are brought to tears at the very thought of you as we cry out to God for you. As a matter of fact, the Lord has shown us visions and given us dreams of you. Our desire is that ALL of our children read this one day and be compelled to join in with us to testify to God's faithfulness. His faithfulness will echo throughout the generations—a chance to step into our pain and yet still see a good Father. A chance to declare His faithfulness even when you cannot see it, to believe in His promises even when the world says they're impossible, and to proclaim His goodness all the while you hope for a river in the desert. I am a miracle child, and you shall be our miracle children. If He can do it for us, He surely will do it again for you.

I am writing this to you in the year 2022 because I have a strong knowing that there will be giants that stand in front of you, and you will need courage and a fatherly reminder to know that your God is faithful and surely is the God of the impossible. Be blessed, my children and future generations, for the Lord **will** show Himself strong on your behalf. For those who believe in Him will never be put to shame. (Romans 10:11)

Table of Contents

Dedication i
Forewords iii
Who Am I Writing This to?................................... ix

CHAPTER 1
    The Beginning..1

CHAPTER 2
    Where Dreams Begin 9

CHAPTER 3
    In the Waiting..20

CHAPTER 4
    Looking Back to Go Forward 34

CHAPTER 5
    The Commute..42

CHAPTER 6
    The First Step..53

CHAPTER 7
    Treasure Hunt..64

CHAPTER 8
    Crazy Faith..78

CHAPTER 9
Grow Your Wings 87

CHAPTER 10
Grace for the Race 106

CHAPTER 11
Legacy is Born 111

1

The Beginning

As the third and youngest child to the most amazing parents on the planet (Dennis and Janie Gallagher), I have felt the Lord's hand upon me all of my life. He has guarded, protected, and guided me every step of the way, and He has no plans to stop now in this faith-taking adventure He has invited me on. The Lord has never failed to direct my steps, even in the times when the next one seemed impossible. It almost seems as if the scarier the journey looks and the bigger the giant gets, the more courage He gives you to conquer it. One of my favorite quotes from a friend of mine is: how can we be more than conquerors and overcomers if we never have anything to overcome or conquer? I love that because

> "How can we be more than conquerors and overcomers if we never have anything to overcome or conquer?"

this goes to tell you that our promise is not that we will never face a battle or have a war, but it is that when the battle comes, and the war knocks at our front door, we have the victory and are more than conquerors in Him—knowing that very truth will birth a warrior in you that never cowers at the site of adversity. Knowing that very truth was something the Lord was teaching me from the jump. Even before all of that, according to the world's prognosis, it was never part of the plan or possible for me to ever be born into this world; at least, that's what they told my father. The enemy attacked, and he attacked hard, but God's will prevailed.

At the age of 32, they told my father he had cancer in a reproductive body part (testicular cancer) and that they had to do an operation that would render him unable to bear children or else the cancer would kill him. The doctor said out of his own mouth, "It would be a miracle for you to ever have children again." He already had a son (my older brother, Josh) at the time, but my dad and mom still desired many more children; for they knew that was the heart of God for their lives. He stood against that report, called upon the Lord, and threw up a "hail-mary" prayer as he sat in his truck one afternoon and prayed his famous "baseball prayer." He cried out, "Lord, all I want to do is see my son play baseball." The Lord surely responded to him. "You shall live and not die."

I can hear it in my spirit, just imagining what the Lord said to my father.

Needless to say, my father is alive and well today. He not only watched his first son play baseball, but he also conceived a daughter almost a month after his surgery, and then many years later, another son (me) that played baseball from a young boy and into college. You see, God's plan triumphed over what the world had to say about his life and body. The Lord writes our future. This was only a precursor miracle that would set the stage for all the miracles God still planned to take place. I know that's a lot to take in just in the first paragraph and start of this book, but it is essential to peer into God's faithfulness for what He has done before you, to have courage in what He is still going to do ahead of you. It's what He does; it's who He is.

Faith in Him grows our wings. As you turn the pages of this book, let God turn the pages of your heart in anticipation that the story in your life isn't finished yet. For this is just the beginning.

Growing up in a house where the presence of the Lord was not hidden or ever hushed had its perks. Late-night prayer meetings, countless Bible studies, and people always praying in some weird language downstairs (the gift of tongues; spiritual language) were a normality at the Gallagher household that showed me my gifts at a very young age. I remember even as a child, I prayed and prayed for a local bar (Leo's bar) behind my parent's house to close down because I knew there was evil taking place there because the Lord had shown me in many dreams. Within a couple of months of praying every night with my dad, the infamous bar that had been there for decades all of the sudden shut down. I think my dad was more shocked than I was when the bar shut down; their parking lot was packed night in and night out. I realize it now, but I did not know then of the true power of intercession. That prayer moves the Hand of God, and the Hand of God moves everything. The Lord answered the prayers of a young boy through fervent prayer, and this was yet just a precursor of greater things to come in the future.

Throughout my adolescent years, the Lord was always on the move with me and in me by simply teaching me. I came to figure out really quickly in my life that I was very sensitive to the Holy Spirit. I was a "feeler." A "feeler" means that when I entered an atmosphere (a geographical place, location, or setting), I would instantly feel which presence was ruling and reigning in that place. For those who are not familiar with the term "feeler," a feeler is a gift that the Lord shares with His sons and daughters despite what age they are. Discernment goes just about hand-in-hand with this gift. Some are born with it, and some eagerly desire and ask the Lord for it, and he answers. In that gift, the Lord will sometimes, in certain scenarios, enable you to feel what is going on in that specific location or even in the man or woman that is near you in that place. Pain, anxiety, hurt, confusion, compassion, physical ailments, worry, and demonic presence are just a few examples of what a feeler will suddenly start to sense and experience. It is the Lord's way of giving you a holy heads-up for what is near and around you. He also will often pair discernment (a knowing in your spirit; a gift of the spirit) with a feeler so that he or she may know the things not seen or the noises not heard. All of that knowledge and revelation is fine and dandy to know now. However, that was not the case when I was just a young boy walking up and down the streets of San Francisco.

I can remember it like it was yesterday; it was my brother's 18th birthday, and we were spending the day out in the Golden City. The day had flashed by, and it was getting late that night while the sun was quickly setting. Just like most 18-year-olds' birthday dreams, he had his mind set on getting a gnarly tattoo. With the night speeding by, we were speed-walking up and down the steep hills of San Francisco, looking for tattoo shops left and right. At last, my brother found one small tattoo shop tucked away in a corner, so my family and I approached it. Immediately, and I mean immediately, young Jake felt a sense of urgency to get out of that area. If I were to paint a better picture of what I felt at that moment, it would be as if an emergency alarm sounded off in my heart, and I started to physically tremble and shake. I ran to my mom's legs and then my dad's leg frantically and kept telling them, "We have to get out of here, we have to get out of here, we have to get out of here." They probably thought I was crazy. I felt like if I did not leave that place, I could possibly die. Unfortunately for me, it didn't look like we were going to be leaving any time soon, as my brother was just taking his time, looking through the tattoo books and trying to pinpoint exactly what he was envisioning. The longer I stayed in that parlor, the stronger the feeling got. It was unrelenting, so much to the point that my mom had to take me outside, kneel down to my level, and ask me, "What is going on?" with a confused expression on her face. I stated, "We cannot be here, we cannot be here," and I meant those words with every bone in my body. She temporarily calmed me down, and we entered the parlor for my brother to make one of his very first big adult decisions.

The terrible feeling kept reoccurring, and I couldn't shake it off. My brother finally decided exactly what he wanted. He rang the bell at the front to notify the worker he was ready. Out from the back of the building, the door slammed, and out came a woman with black, frizzy old hair, tattoos all over her body, glossed-over eyes, piercings everywhere the eye could see, and most of all, a countenance on her face that I as a young kid had never seen before. It was like her eyes were open, but I could not tell if she was awake. She got to the front desk, leaned over the end of it, and asked my brother, "What are we going to get you today, young man?"

As she spoke, I just knew something was not right and that evil was heavily in the room. Now, it wasn't just any tattoo that my brother wanted; it was actually a very specific one. He told her, "I want a tattoo of three sharp nails on top of each other."

Her response was, "Ooooh, I really like that," (in a really creepy voice). Then he resumed saying, "I want the nails to be scarlet nails that have blood dripping on the tips of them." She happily responded, "Oooh, I really, really like that," (as if the word, blood, had pleased her). Lastly, he said, "I also want a cross etched out behind the nails dripping with blood." She asked, "What does the cross stand for?" He replied, "It stands for the Lord Jesus Christ who was hung on the cross for my sins with three nails where his blood was shed for me."

When she heard that last part of what my brother had said, she yelled and shrieked, like a demon had woken up in her—something I'd never experienced before.

She strongly insisted that he should not get that tattoo, but he persisted; for he knew what he wanted in his heart. At that point, my parents took me outside because my body was trembling and trembling. After all, I was feeling the demonic activity in the room that they were now aware of. Oddly enough, shortly after, my brother followed my parents outside the tattoo parlor in pure frustration; he had forgotten his driver's license and could not prove he was 18 to get the tattoo. My brother may have felt frustrated, but I, on the other hand, felt like I could finally breathe. "Get me the heck out of this place," was what I thought as we finally walked away. What I felt that night in that eerie San Francisco tattoo parlor was a feeling I continued to experience as my youth turned to adulthood. It was a bookmark for me that served as a reference point for future chapters in my life. I continued to grow into my gift as a feeler and am still growing in it to this very day. For the Lord had revealed to me that He lets me in on these feelings, emotions, and atmospheres so that I would not be overwhelmed and succumb to them but rather activate prayer/intercession and walk in my heavenly authority. As a feeler, you can either partner with heaven and His glory or succumb to darkness and its story. My life as a "feeler" and my sensitivity to the spirit has played a crucial role in several steps in my life and will continue to unfold in this book as the Lord grows my wings in this faith-filled journey.

As a matter of fact, if this gift hadn't been in operation, my wife and I, in years to come, probably never would have been able to see the place He was leading us—the place where our dreams would begin.

2

Where Dreams Begin

"Grow my wings" is a phrase that you have already seen stated a couple of times from the beginning of this book. What does it mean? Where does it come from? And how does it play out in this story? To fully understand the reason this phrase strikes the very core of my being is for many revelations that this story will shed light on and connect together, chapter by chapter. For me to help you see what I saw and go where I went, I would first have to invite you into a life-changing encounter that I certainly will remember every detail of until my life on this earth is complete.

Come with me; I want to invite you to my very first glimpse of what it means to "grow my wings." It did not happen while I was awake; it had transpired in the midnight hour as a young kid lay in his bed and dreamed his most real dream yet to date. As I slept, I dreamed a dream that felt more real than anything before. In this dream, I was sitting on a computer chair in the loft of my parent's house, praising and worshipping the Lord with my hands raised as music played. As I praised and worshipped, the roof of the house cracked in the middle, split in two, and opened up, fully becoming removed from the house.

As this occurred, I felt a feeling I could only describe as if "His glory had caught me up into the sky." I ascended high into the air and atmosphere, and was placed right next to countless flying eagles as far as the eye could see. Anyone else had flying dreams before? Truly an indescribable feeling. These eagles were flying all in the same direction, in a linear fashion, with their wings spread wide, making the piercing sound and triumphant noise that only they do. As I looked up to where we were going, we were flying directly into the sun. The dream ended, and I woke up with a joy so unspeakable. I rushed down the stairs as fast as I could to tell my parents the dream, but all I could remember that came out of my mouth was, "I was flying, I was flying, I was flying with the eagles."

That night, I dreamed in my life what many people would call a "God dream." I didn't know then that this dream would be carried with me all my life, but I do now. The Lord began to download revelations into my heart of what he had shown me and what He was calling me in my life. Weeks after that, I discovered my favorite Bible verse that quickly became my life anthem even still till this day—Isaiah 40:31, For those that wait on the Lord, he will renew their strength, they will mount up on wings like eagles. They will walk and not grow weary; they shall run and not faint. This right here is where "Growing my wings" officially began.

> "For those that wait on the Lord, he will renew their strength, they will mount up on wings like eagles. They will walk and not grow weary; they shall run and not faint."
> *Isaiah 40:31*

As I continued in my journey of life as a young man, the Lord wasted no time in showing me that I was called to set myself apart. 2 Corinthians 6:17 says it this way—"Therefore, come out from among them and be separate, says the Lord." Talking about setting yourself apart and not becoming like everyone around you. Another scripture (Romans 12:2) echoes a similar truth, saying, "Do not be conformed to the ways of this world, but be transformed by the renewing of your mind, that you may prove what is that good, and acceptable, and perfect, will of God." Not only in my dream was I called to rise up, separate myself, and fly with the eagles, but also in my daily life, the Lord showed me the same. He was calling me to be different, and I felt it. I started off in a private Christian school where I was taught biblical truths and godly principles and fostered in an atmosphere to grow in Christ—something I'll forever be thankful for. That time ran its course, and my parents lacked the funds to continue, but they quickly knew that I'd find just as much success in public school as I found in private school. Public elementary school came, and I had no appetite to do the things everyone else was doing. Although I did excel in sports, academics, and awards, not to mention I also had no shortage of people to be around because of my athletic relationships. However, even in all of that, something was off. I knew what I wanted for my life, and I knew doing what everyone else was doing certainly was not going to get me there. Since that dream, a greater conviction has come upon me. Nothing that my peers ever did attracted me or looked desirable. I believe the Lord protected me in many ways just by giving me a holy appetite for lasting fruit in my life.

High school quickly followed, and the pressure became stronger to be like everyone else; to cave in and conform to the culture, yet the spirit within me was never satisfied with that. At the events and parties that my sports teams would throw after games, I would often be the only one or of the few not to partake or go. There was nothing lasting that was there for me. Many people like to use this time of their lives to "experiment," but I once again had a conviction within me that kept me from pursuing that and going down that road. At that time, my mom also broke the "I have breast cancer" news at the dinner table one night to the family. I can remember it like it was yesterday. The air was sucked out of the room as my heart slowly broke. I didn't even get to finish my dinner that night; for my appetite left quicker than the fork coming down from my mouth and hitting my plate. It provoked the fear of God in me to not waste another second of my life that I had on this earth. I knew then that my life and time would not be wasted with the worthless things the world had to offer me. David, in the Bible, says it like this, "Teach me Lord to number my days, so that I may gain a heart of wisdom (Psalms 90:12)."

You ever get hit with those moments where life just happens to you? This was one of those times. My very first one. One thing about the hard times in my life is that they only compelled me to want to get closer to the Lord and draw near to the Eternal Flame, Jesus. I prayed for my mom consistently; I even held her in my arms while she wept, and my dad shaved her head bald through chemotherapy treatment. She cried in my arms because she thought she was vulnerable and defeated, but I saw that she was brave and beautiful. God was my only refuge, and I knew He was my mom's as well at that time.

I remember that after dinner that night, I ran up into my room and did not want to go forward one more inch in life. I didn't want to go to basketball. What was there for me to do at school, and how could I just go on normally living my day-to-day life, all the while knowing my mom was being beaten down and suffering from cancer? I couldn't. My perspective changed. My thoughts changed. My mindset had a whole new focus. Things no longer mattered; not one bit. I remember my mom saw that I was defeated and hurt by this in a devastating way that night of the dinner. She knocked on my door, came to my room, grabbed my hands, and made me a deal. "If I don't give up, you can't give up either! Promise me?" she insisted with tears in her eyes. It hit me; if she could have the courage like that through this valley of the shadow of death, surely could I! Courage hit me like a ton of bricks and infused me like never before. This tragedy caused me to run even harder after the Lord than I already was. King Solomon says something like this, The name of the Lord is a strong tower; the righteous run to it and are made safe (Proverbs 18:10). We ran hard.

> "The name of the Lord is a strong tower; the righteous run to it and are made safe."
> *Proverbs 18:10*

Who are you running to? He was the only One who could help me and the only One I was going to be running to. He made me safe. I ran, I ran, and I ran hard. I ran to Him and sought to rally with God-fearing men at that time, but even the "Christians" (quoted for a reason) that I wanted to grow close to and rally together in faithfulness and righteousness were one foot in and one foot out every other day, it seemed like. One day, they were on the stage with a microphone in the church, but the next day at school, partaking in sin, lies, and a life that was consumed by selfishness. It ruined my appetite and left a bad taste in my mouth. It left me disappointed.

I knew in my heart to stay humble and not think that I was better than anyone else just because I wanted more for my life. However, I just KNEW that God was calling me to fly higher. I knew right away that true faithfulness and true righteousness to follow the Lord was my only reasonable sacrifice, not to live a perfect life, but to live a life worthy of what He died for. In my mind's eye, I thought to myself, "Why would I ever live this life that He has given me just to fake it like I'm really serving him? I wasn't going to fool Him, and I definitely wasn't fooling myself. I knew it was either I was all in or I was all out; I chose the first option, for the Lord and, quite honestly, for my mom at that time. My whole life changed.

The Lord never promises a challenge-free or easy life, but He does promise that the pain you will walk through doesn't have to be a journey you take alone. College quickly jumped on the scene, and baseball was my passion, which I pursued all the way to the very end. I found joy in the game, character through its lessons, humility through its failures, triumph in its victories, and even determination through its many injuries. Although the joy of the game was tangible, and its future was promising, I've had tastes of joy even greater, and that joy was in the presence of the Lord. In a location of massive church billboards, corporate churches all around, and plenty of mega churches, I met the true presence of the Lord sitting under pots and pans inside a Stockton house. Profound healings, unexplainable miracles, and a tangible presence of the Lord that moved my heart were happening every week I went. During that time, the Lord even used me to pray for and heal a lady's broken leg at one of those evening gatherings, and I didn't even know I could do that. The Lord did it through me. An awakening occurred in me, and I saw the more; the more that He had for His people, the more that He had for my family, and the more that he had for me. My whole paradigm of who and what I thought of God had to be re-worked and rooted from the ground up. I started praying for people everywhere that I went. At school, the grocery store, the movie theatres, and the baseball field, I began to step out, and the Lord was healing people! I felt like a superhero who just figured out his super-power for the first time. Humbly, it had nothing to do with me and everything to do with Him! As time went on over the years, I let go of collegiate baseball (the hardest decision of my life at that time) to pursue a local leadership school.

Although it did not make sense to many people at that time, for I had many schools inquiring of me. I was getting scouted by the Braves, but I knew I had to follow what my heart was being called to, or I would regret it. I was in a place of a huge tug of war between my mind and my spirit.

In my time of great sacrifice to let go, the Lord gave me a greater reward to take hold of.

This was a lesson I'm glad I learned then because I would need to cling to this truth in the future to come. He was already teaching me that through sacrifice to Him, He would show up and show off on my behalf, and He did just that. (Side note: The Lord will never force you to do something; He is not a controlling God or a manipulative Father. He provokes you and compels you in your spirit to follow him and obey His leading, but ultimately, you CHOOSE if you will listen or not. He moves your spirit, but you move your legs). Funny enough, soon after I let go of baseball and pursued a leadership school, I ran into Rebekah Bonds (the girl I sat next to in the 5th grade) at the gym. My eyes lit up as I saw her on that day. She may say I was shaking because I was nervous about talking to her, but I was shaking because it was my first workout in a month. I invited her to church, we re-connected, hung out a couple of times, blinked, and just like that, the rest was history. She donned a beautiful shiny ring indicating our promise to each other in 2018. Easiest decision of my life.

Fast forward to the year 2020, which was here. Rebekah and I had just gotten married a few months prior (October 19th, 2019). COVID (a global pandemic virus) came on the scene, the entire world shut down, we both lost our jobs, and we quickly moved out of our first apartment together, right into my parent's loft where I, as a kid, dreamed my

God dream. It was not quite the newlywed start we were looking for. Not quite the honeymoon phase that everyone was talking about … Everything we thought about our lives and our future all went out the window, and everything came to a screeching halt. Not to mention, my father and I got falsely accused by a company we were both working for, and we not only lost our job to COVID but also got sent a cease and desist because "we knew too much about the business." He was the general-manager, and I was promised as the "bright and shining face of the future" of a well-oiled machine, multi-million-dollar company. It almost felt like our lives were beginning and ending at the same time in every way possible. Life was "just happening" to us from every angle and at every turn. Has anyone ever felt like that? I know I did. When it rains, it pours they say.

Nonetheless, the Lord was keeping us and holding us in His hands; all the while, all we could see was despair. I remember many nights asking the Lord, "Why? Why? How could you be letting all of this happen to me, Lord? How could my father and I, righteous ones who serve you, be falsely accused and dirt thrown at us?" It seemed like the enemy was winning. The business world, as many people may have experienced possibly reading this, that people will burn you in the most opportune moments they get. However, the Lord sees every injustice on earth, and He fights for His children. For what the enemy meant for evil against me, surely the Lord would turn it for good (Genesis 50:20). It was only a matter of time. God knew what He was doing; for new passions and desires began to well up within us—my wife and I. New longings began to birth, and a heart for new territory began to germinate within our hearts. Out of a season of sorrow filled with tears, those tears were the very thing watering the seed to come. This chapter is called "Where Dreams Begin," and as you can see many times, the inception of a dream is not always glamorous or pretty. It is not delivered in stunning wrapping paper and a perfect bow on your front porch. Many of them begin out of the nightmares and tragedies of life. That gladness is grown out of the soil of sorrow. Seasons of beauty come from the season of ashes we walk through. Seasons of mourning are just a trigger point for the season of joy right around the bend, and seasons of breakdown are just precursors to the season of breakthrough. That same desert you are walking through is also a riverbed waiting to happen. Those tears that you have sowed, you shall also reap with songs of joy. For a new season that we had entered, one we had never felt before. Faith, courage, and a little bit of crazy would propel us into the next thing God already had in mind for us. There was a feeling we couldn't shake, a thought we could not stop thinking about, and a drawing that would not stop tugging at our hearts. Our spirits were experiencing it, but we had yet to see anything happen in the natural. All we could do was wait.

3

In the Waiting

Between the promise and the pain, there is something called process. Process: the place you go through that is not glamorous, it's not fun, it's very monotonous—the seemingly insignificant mundane land that you must pass through to taste a promise. Often overlooked, this very place is the destination where many people give in, throw in the towel, retreat to where they came from (like the Israelites wanting to go back to Egypt), renounce their faith, and sometimes even the place many people are tempted to fall away in the faith totally. Looking at the word of God, we can see that the place of process is actually almost like a gift from God.

Correction: it's not "like the gift" he gives us; it "is the gift" he gives us. He gives it to His children so that we can become ready to hold the promise He has for us. Many times, the weight of the promise He desires to give to us weighs too much for people to hold if it is out of season or not the right time. For Joseph, the process was the prison before the palace. For David, it was the shepherd boy in the wilderness before the kingdom at his fingertips. For Daniel, it was the Lion's den before his renowned influence. For Jesus, it was 30 years of life before His ministry and first miracle. For Noah, it was his faithfulness to preach 120 years in a perverse generation, and only seven people (his family) entered the ark before the flooding of the ark. For Moses, it was the season of frustration and righteous anger that would raise a deliverer. For Abraham, it was being faithful to leave everything so that the Lord could give him anything. You get the point. My wife and I stepped heel-deep into a season of process and waiting, and if I was being honest with you today, it was excruciating. Not only have we tasted on our lips the beauty of being married, alone, joined together, and building our lives together for about 11 months, but we were just getting comfortable in our marriage routine. Then, bang! In the blink of an eye, we were loading up car after car, moving right back in with family. What seemed like a setback … a huge setback. Little did we know in hindsight, this would be the very launching pad that the Lord had rolled up His sleeve.

When you look back at the scripture verse, Isaiah 40:31, "For those that wait on the Lord, he will renew their strength, they will mount up on wings like eagles. They will walk and not grow weary; they shall run and not faint," you see a word there that is not all too exciting to the naked eye. The first seven words of that verse are: "For those who

WAIT on the Lord!" I know you saw it there in all caps. Let me spell it out again … "WAIT!" If only you just "wait on Him," he will do all the following in that verse: The word "wait" is mentioned 139 times throughout the books of the Bible, and surely enough, my wife and I were about to find out why. Could the word "wait" have some significance to it? Carried more significance than we once thought? Maybe waiting on the Lord has a different meaning than what the world has always told us.

Waiting on the Lord is not merely just sitting around with your feet kicked back in a recliner, lethargically expecting the Lord to drop something in your lap. Waiting on the Lord is not stagnant; it is not lazy, and it doesn't have to be a place of instability. In addition, it surely is not the place to forfeit what you have been believing and contending for. Rather, waiting is the test. I loved this quote I heard which stated: The Lord is waiting on you to see what you do while you're waiting on Him. You might want to read that one again. He is watching closely to see your response in these kinds of seasons. Are you dropping your sword during this time, or are you still raising it? Are you walking past the armor of God at your front door, or is it still the first thing you're putting on when the dawn awakens? Are you still burning that midnight oil,

> **"The Lord is waiting on you to see what you do while you're waiting on Him."**

or must your lampstand be dusted off? Are you cursing your current situation because you don't understand it, or are you prophesying to your future by remembering the promises He gave you? Are you still declaring that He is faithful toward you, or are you wallowing in the bait of Satan that steals your ear and says, "Maybe He isn't as good as you thought He was?" This is the place where you don't allow your next move to be based on circumstance but by faith alone. God feeds the birds but He doesn't throw the worms into the nest. I'm fully convinced that waiting is the invitation where you either gain or surrender territory in your life. You have a choice; you either take it or give it up. I would urge you to merge your faith with action in these times. For it very well could be that your greatest place of warfare, in due time, will become your greatest place of inheritance. It's your choice.

With that said, waiting on the Lord for us looked like looking for jobs, getting settled in again with my parents, praying to the Lord morning and night, exercising, and then waiting again. We would go on prayer walks around my childhood neighborhood, praying over our destinies and speaking life over our current situation, even though we didn't like it or merely understood it. I don't know if any of you reading this today have ever been in the season or position of your life where you absolutely know that the Lord listens to your prayers, but you feel like you're hitting brass heavens. This usually happens in combination with when you're smack dab right in the middle of the process.

Granted, you're not habitually sinning and separating yourself from Him. But nothing is happening, nothing is working, you're not hearing anything, you are not feeling anything, you have no dreams to guide you, and you feel totally forgotten, with a complete lack of direction. I know some of you have been there; maybe some of you are there right now as you're reading this. All there is left to do is wait. Unfortunately, in the hustle and bustle, climbing the corporate ladder, and stepping on top of your opponent's head to get to the top kind of world, we know very little about resting, waiting, and process.

If you have walked with the Lord for quite some time, you are bound to stand toe-to-toe with these moments. Some call them the desert or valley season; just like a desert and wilderness, you are painfully thirsting for His voice and will at all costs. It's like you'd do anything just to get a drop of His refreshing water or just to hear Him say even one word that sets it all straight. Remember this today: that place is the invitation. I love reading the Bible (especially the Psalms) because David in the wilderness and the trying seasons helps us realize that we were not the only ones that faced this kind of thing. The man who God claims to be a man after God's heart in Psalms 22:1 says it like this, "My God, My God why have you forsaken me? Why are you so far from helping me, and from the words of my groaning? O My God, I cry in the daytime, but You do not hear, and in the night seasons, and am not silent." He also goes on to say, "My heart is like wax; it has melted within Me. My strength is dried up." As if that wasn't enough, Psalms 61 says, "My soul longs for you in a dry and thirsty land."

As you can see, David was all too familiar with this place, but trust me, the story doesn't end there. He is there with you, and His silence is not His absence. Ultimately, what do you do in a dry and thirsty land? Well, you pray for the river in the desert. That river is the Lord and the breakthrough that He brings with His mighty right hand. Isaiah 43:19 says, "Behold, I will do a new thing, now it shall spring forth; Shall you not know it? I will even make a road in the wilderness *and* **rivers in the desert.**" Declare that truth. He will do a new thing in His perfect timing, and in that dry and thirsty land, He will surely burst through as the river in the desert.

Before David became king, he was just some little shepherd boy tending his flock year after year. Shunned by his own father, an outcast to his family, thrown off into the fields, therein lays a very non-glamorous invitation. Somewhere between a giant falling and a king being anointed in the presence of his enemies, there was a man just waiting. In his waiting, he was slaying lions and bears. In his waiting, he was worshiping with his harp. In his waiting, he wrote letters and psalms that glorified the Lord that we sing today. In his waiting, he was slinging stones. In his waiting, he was rescuing the lost sheep back to their rightful position. It was all in his waiting. So, what does "waiting" look like? Just by looking at David, we know waiting looks like standing. Waiting looks like declaring His truth, fighting in faith, honing your God-given abilities, and going to war in worship and song. You wait, you wait, and you wait again, and then it happens. He does a new thing. "Behold I will do a new thing, **now** it shall spring forth!" For my wife and I, we knew it, and we felt it. He certainly was doing a new thing; we didn't quite know about the timing part yet.

It wouldn't be crazy to say that He was doing a new thing in just about everybody's life during this time. You either had to rely on the government's free money to pay your way, or you were forced to pivot your life to change the trajectory of all you ever knew. Many people started businesses, some opened up their own schools, some quickly jumped to online forms of profit (influencers, YouTube channels, live-streaming, etc.), and some finally took a shot at their dreams that a 9 to 5 prohibited them from pursuing. The only question to remain during this time was, "Is your ear tuned in to hearing His voice?" As many people in this time (the year 2020) had known or maybe you reading this are just hearing about it, it seemed that just about everyone had been temporarily laid off or completely lost their jobs. Jobs seemed to be a luxury as the world stood paralyzed in fear with a world-wide virus outbreak. From every small business on your downtown strip to even the business giants and corporations of the world, people were out of work and, more so—out of whack. According to the world leaders, it was deemed "too dangerous" to work or be near people.

Nonetheless, an opportunity arose, and I took this job in the Greater Bay Area. Right from the get-go, I was able to take big strides and make huge impact. This was the start of something. The Lord had opened a door for me. However, this door of opportunity came not only at a high salary but also at a high price, physically, and mentally. The location of this site I would be on required me to travel a little under 200 miles a day and sit in traffic at lengths as great as 5-7 hours a day, on top of a full workday. In hindsight, I could tell you all of that, but after accepting the job at first, I had no idea what I was getting myself into or what this meant for me. The title of this chapter is probably starting to make sense to you now. "In the waiting" in traffic was about to become uncomfortably familiar. I started this job and started making the daunting drive through the waves of traffic on a day-to-day basis. Even though it was extremely rigorous, the Lord was putting favor on me in my workplace, not just by working hard but also by praying for people in the midst of a worldwide crisis. At this time, my wife was staying at home, still looking for jobs, and trying to find her way with her next endeavor, but it just wasn't happening for her. She would look, try, pray, and take a step outside her comfort zone, and no door would budge. She didn't know it then, but we sure do understand now that doors were being blocked for a specific reason. I was working extremely hard, and she was at a standstill. It's like she and I were in polar opposite seasons just like that, in the blink of an eye. I would wake up at 3 a.m., work for a full day, and drive for just about a full day. The amount of time this lasted was just under one year. Between the promise and the process for me, there was something called "the commute."

As time went on, mornings seemed to arrive quicker, the days got harder, the drives got longer, and the confusion and frustration of what God's next step was for us became more and more distant. Kind of like David in Psalms 22 when he said, "Why are you so far from me, helping me and from the words of my groaning?" That's how I felt. During this time, the Lord was working on my wife's heart and mine to pursue all He had for us and not settle for just the "good." So, we simply threw up a prayer and told Him, "Lord, we want to experience all that you have for us and our futures; where is that? If that is here in California or elsewhere, please reveal it to us." That was a pretty dangerous question and prayer because the Lord is definitely in the business of giving crazy answers to crazy prayers.

A little back story before jumping too far ahead: Rebekah and I never once batted an eye or even winked at ever moving our lives. Not once, not when we were dating, not much when we were engaged, and maybe counting on a couple of fingers when we got married. As a matter of fact, it was a conversation I often shut down because our futures looked pretty solidified and rooted in where we were. Why would we? How could we? It just wouldn't make sense.

Rebekah spent most of her entire adolescent years raising and babysitting her niece and going to college while her sister worked, and I, for the most part, have a best friend in my dad that I'd never want to leave, plus a bucket load of nieces and nephews on both sides. Our heart for family and children is no shock to anyone who knows us. It's no secret we love our family. It wouldn't even do justice for us to say that we are huge "family people." If you could look up the phrase "family people" in the dictionary, the faces of my wife and I would be right there smack dab for all to see. There was never a weekend we had free where we weren't at a family party, a family dinner, a family function, someone's birthday, or merely just around family celebrating something going on in our lives. We did not just love our families; they were everything and still are. Therefore, moving away from everything we knew and everything we loved was never conceivable. Not only that, but nobody in our families really knew anything different. We've always been in the same spot, and no one ever thought differently. We were where we were, and that was it. Except two people … my grandpa and grandma, Dave and Gwen Gallagher. I can write a whole book about them. However, I'm going to get back to them later. They were trailblazers, pioneers, and people who, by all means, expanded territory.

So, as you can see, moving away from home, or even crazier to a land we have never even seen or stepped on, would have been crazy. Until it wasn't. So, there it was, one evening after one of the longest days I had driving and working, I walked up the stairs, greeted my wife with a kiss, and there it was, she had this conviction about her. She had a different look in her eyes and a countenance that seemed to have changed from being disappointed and down to excited and giddy. She looked at me with life in her captivating green eyes, which I prayed for, and with a little ounce of nervousness in her voice, she said, "Let's move to Texas!" "Texas?" I replied. "Yes, Texas!" she continued. I asked her, "Why there and what for?" This was the interesting part. She didn't really know. It wasn't like she spun the fifty states wheel of fortune blindfolded, shot an arrow, and there it was, it landed on Texas. No, there was something about her statement that indicated she was sure and surprisingly excited. This is what she knew—"I feel like there's something there for us, and that we are being called, not just for us but for the children we are going to have," she stated. That definitely hit me from way out of left field, especially after such a long day, but for some odd reason, it undeniably struck my core.

It was so intentional that we were to move there from her perspective. Yes, we spent our fair share of time looking at houses on the internet within different states. We have definitely watched some TV shows with Texas in them, but that was all super casual and insignificant compared to thinking about uprooting our lives to be there. We knew not one person, had not one family member or friend that had been there. We had never seen it, stepped foot on its soil, or entertained the idea before, but here we were, looking at each other, knowing we were both crazy because we felt something in our spirits jump. The curiosity was birthed in this moment but placed there by the Holy Spirit. It began to become a frequent topic of conversation for us. While we were driving in the car, in the mornings with our cup of coffee, at night before we'd go to bed, on phone calls throughout the day, sometimes we'd even casually throw it out there to our families to see how they would react. There was one thing for sure, and it was that every time we heard the word "Texas," our spirits leaped in an indescribable way. A seed was planted.

The next step ahead was that we definitely needed to seek counsel and pray for the Father to reveal this to us clearly and plainly. The word clearly tells us in: Proverbs 15:22, Without counsel, plans go awry (wrong), but in the multitude of counsel they are established. Do you have people in your life you can trust? Can you count on them to intercede for you? Do you have people praying about God's best for your life? And I'm not talking about the people who say they'll pray for you after you tell them your struggles, and they casually leave your conversation on to the next thing (you and that person both know they aren't going to be praying for you). I'm talking about the people who check in on you, ask you questions about follow-up prayers, contend with you, ask you how you are doing, send you scriptures, and profess them over your life, and they are STANDING with you both in word and deed for God's plan and counsel over your life.

When I envision the word "contend," my mind takes me to a picture of two warriors on a battlefield. As they stand back-to-back, hand-and-hand, and sword-to-sword, they fight together, protecting each other as the enemy attacks on all sides. This is the same picture of exactly what we need in our prayer lives as well. When we ask for prayer and counsel, this is the invitation we are extending. If you don't have these people in your life, I strongly suggest you think about it, for it will save you worlds of trouble! Pray for the Lord to bring the right people into your life. You'd be surprised to know that people can see things that you could never see a mile away. We didn't want to move prematurely because we wanted it, but ultimately, if we ever did do it, it would be because He wanted it. I think many times we fall into situations where we, in our own strength and desires, say the Lord is "telling us to do something."

However, in reality, it's what we wanted for ourselves, which would be better than where we currently are. There's always going to be "the grass is greener over here" moments for all of us in our lives, but no patch of green grass is worth going to that He's not on. I don't want to be where He's not. I don't want to go where He's not leading because when we go against the grain of His will, we end up in places where we are leaning on our own strength and where His grace (the empowering hand of God that pushes us forward) is removed. When His grace isn't there, it starts to seem like the things that were once so easy to do are now so difficult to accomplish. This happens, and it unfortunately brings us to a place where we took what seemed to be 1 step forward but only to be three steps back in the blink of an eye. This was because it wasn't His will, and His signature wasn't on it. I know that the greatest display of love I could give to my King is obedience to where He was calling me and letting Him be my leader.

We didn't want to just up and move without the Lord's hand showing us and His voice leading us. We needed to know beyond a shadow of a doubt that He was prompting this and that He was wrapped all around it. Signs, wonders, confirmations, and dreams would have to be present for the Lord to do such a thing in us and, quite honestly, for us to even have enough courage to do it. We asked for them and prayed for them continually. Now, Rebekah and I have asked several leaders in our lives to pray with us about this move and give us counsel. We did this continually as we carried this desire that we believed the Lord wanted to birth through us. But before I could move forward with anything else, I thought to myself, "who in my life do I know that's even done something like this? Do I know anyone? "What did they learn? Did they regret it?" At first, I thought my memory wasn't serving me well, but then, "duh," I thought to myself, look no further than my own family themselves. Grandpa and Grandma Gallagher.

4

Looking Back to Go Forward

The only people I knew maybe I could talk to were none other than my beloved grandpa and grandma, David and Gwendolyn Gallagher. Earlier, when I told you that I could write a book on them, that was the truest of true statements, and maybe I will one day. They are no longer with us as I am currently writing this story, but my goodness, did they ever so brand my heart with their love and direction in their final fleeting moments of life! My grandpa had a profound impact on my life.

Gwendolyn graduated to heaven on December 24th, 2020, and my Grandpa Dave shortly followed her home a little over a year later on January 17th, 2022. Both were dying with their loving families all around them in the comforts of their own homes, and there were some things that they said (especially my grandpa) before their passing that I know now have altered my entire life forever—and not just my life and my wife's but also my children's whom I'm writing to. This beautiful picture-perfect story book of love between my grandparents was nothing short of extraordinary. David Gallagher was a war pilot, cryptographer, and engineer who valiantly served his country in WWII with the Army Air Force. He crash-landed in the Fiji Islands, miraculously survived, and lived to see the day when he'd fall in love with a nurse girl named Gwendolyn Marjorie Roley. I told you it was a movie. My father and I actually stumbled upon a journal entry that he wrote called "***Pilots Halo***"—something he wrote himself that no one knew about, and that we joyfully discovered after his passing. This story pens to real life what ran through a young David Gallagher's brain as he was experiencing what he thought to be the last moments of his beloved life. They comprised the moments he saw with his very own two eyes before the crash landing in the Fiji Islands.

His "Pilots Halo" entry goes like this, *"My memory goes back 70 years when I was in the 149 AACS Squadron flying in the Solomon Island area August 1946. I can visualize floating, drifting in a noisy, loud roar of two Pratt and Whitneys (engines of the plane) at 6,000 feet, surrounded by floating, drifting white, grey clouds with a background of soft blue skies peeking through my white, grey cloud buddies. Yep! The clouds are my buddy because they are the only thing there except old B-25 Miss Lovely (name of the plane). Through the engine roar, I feel somewhat peaceful until I hear that engine sputter and sputter. I did not get excited because it does that all the time to wake me up. Kinda scarry and peaceful at the same time. Just like a movie screen, in and out, in and out as the clouds change from near to far, but the shadow stayed constant. What does a 20-year-old farm boy know about this, I hadn't ever traveled more than 50 miles from home until now. Wait, all of a sudden I see a large, colorful light, 360-degree circle around the shadow of Miss Lovely (the B-25 American medium bomber aircraft). You ask, am I nuts, delusional, or am I dreaming? It is getting brighter; by golly, that is a rainbow. The rainbows one downside up and one downside down, full circle. I hope that memory was real, thus proving I am sane and not nuts. I don't care if my God has played a trick on me. Thank you, God. Anyhow, I enjoyed that scene and memory. I didn't know pilots enjoyed that 360-degree shadow rainbow show. After all, floating through the sky in a big hunk of aluminum for a living does have its rewards. You are really out here 600 miles of ocean with nothing but a deep ocean below to enhance the view. Okay, the fat lady just sang."*

Now, the miracle of this very beautiful and personal story of my grandfather shows the mighty right hand of the Lord that was in his life. David Gallagher survived that plane crash as he soared over the Solomon Islands in an effort to get to his destination. He suffered jungle rot and damage to his ear drum that day that he, unfortunately, ended up battling with for the rest of his life. Nonetheless, he lived. In a crash that should have left him dead, he quickly became the living evidence of a complete miracle. If his life had not been spared, neither my father nor I, nor any of my family for that matter, would be alive today. I hope you enjoyed this entry of his; for I know I shed a tear when I first read it. It's always humbling and sobering to peek into history and see even what the Lord did in a time when you weren't alive yet. The amazing part of this miraculous beauty of a story is not just that he survived that day, but that even in his old age (70 years later), he recalled that experience detail for detail of what "a young 20-year-old farm boy" saw that day. His memory was sharp and keen even till his old age, something that always amazed me.

Thank you, Lord, for keeping him alive on that day; for my life is now an extension of your faithfulness to my grandpa. From generation to generation, you are faithful, and you reading this today, see the evidence of this. David Gallagher survived that day for more reasons than one, but no more important than meeting his beautiful wife, Gwendolyn. Dave met the love of his life, Ms. Gwennie, at a Memorial Day ballroom dance, of course. When asked for a way to contact her after the dance, she looked at him and said, "Look it up in the phonebook; I'm the only Roley in it." There was something about that blue dress and the magical way fate worked its magic that night. You probably get

> "my life is now an extension of your faithfulness to my grandpa."

where this story is going. You're right; they danced their way into history for decades to come.

Their life was a movie; their hearts were pure, their quiver was full to the brim with five children, and they gave me my best friend, my dad (Dennis Gallagher). After serving his country courageously and selflessly, David came home, got his education, and graduated from Kansas University (KU). He swiftly married his dream girl, Gwennie, and settled up with their five kids in Missouri for most of their lives, where he accepted an engineering management position at the great General Motors (GM). They laid their roots there for the time being, and then there came a moment when his job offered him a daring position. It was a position that was located in California—a plant engineer management position. This kind of leap of faith would thrust them into a place they had never been, never visited, or previously thought of. And sure enough, after much prayerful consideration, they decided to do something crazy! I remember that before his passing, I had told him that I had strong feelings and an undeniable urge to move to Texas. However, I was struggling with the tug-of-war of it all. My heart strings were being pulled left and right on the daily. My spirit would shout "Yes," and then my mind would suppress it with a harsh "No." It felt like there was never a winning option. Grabbing hold of a new thing meant letting go of a familiar thing; traveling into new lands meant leaving the stomping grounds my shoes knew so well. Also, moving in order to start my family would mean I would be leaving the family I already had all around me. My heart was torn. So, what did I do? I visited the hero himself!

I visited my grandpa quite often. However, I knew the time I had with him was fleeting quickly, especially with the way he was holding up mentally and physically after the love of his life's passing. He was fragile and hurting, but if he were around you, he would never let you see that or show any sign of believing that. That's just how he was. I remember talking to him about these thoughts and emotions that were weighing on me one evening as I visited him in his Manteca house. I asked him, "how did you do it? What pushed you over the hump to accept that job and move across the country? How did you know?" Laughingly, he responded with an answer that seemed to be easy: It wasn't an easy task, but I knew if we didn't do it, we would've regretted it. Boom. That one struck me like lightning. I thought to myself, "my goodness, that's what I have been feeling all along." I knew deep down in my heart that I would regret not going to Texas. I knew that those words alone impacted me if that was all he had to say about it. He didn't stop there; he then also mentioned to me that "just because something is hard or painful does not mean that it's not something you should do." He backed it up with a story.

> "If we didn't do it, we would've regretted it."

"When Gwen and I left Saint Joseph, Missouri there were over 250 people at our going away party as we drove away in our car. Each and every person had tears in their eyes as we waved goodbye with them in our rearview. Not only that, but at this time, we already had all 5 of our children, and our families were all actively a part of their lives in huge ways. Aunties were losing their nieces, uncles were losing their nephews, and we were leaving everything. It was devastating" (all the things I've been thinking about). "Nonetheless, we left, did it, and never looked back. It was a dream only Gwen and I could see. Now look, everyone's in California," he laughed! "We all moved here to California, and what if everyone all moved to Texas where you were one day?" he stated. "I could see that happen," as he smirked at me. The conversation ended, and we casually transitioned into some family banter about the war or some old wild western film he wanted me to watch as we did so often (any of my cousins, brother, or sister reading this know exactly what I'm talking about).

After that day, anytime my grandpa would see me, he would say, "Hey, big TX," or "Hey, there's big TX," or "How are you doing, big TX?" as if he was saying something he knew already that I didn't. I'm sure he did. He was prophesying. After that talk with him that day, I continued my visits with him frequently, but he was deteriorating at a rapid pace and later on graduated to heaven. Throughout all the sorrow and despair of his passing, in his fleeting moments, he gave me the greatest gift … only a gift he could give because he knew exactly what it was to have it—the gift of courage. After talking with him, I left his house with a different pep in my step and confidence in my stride. Faith had consumed me, kind of like at the beginning of the book when my mom told me that I couldn't give up because she wasn't going to when she waged war on the diagnosis of breast cancer. As it was then, so it was now. After talking with Grandpa, it was like my mind and heart could do one big, long exhale because everything that he said was everything I needed to hear. I miss him every day that passes by. Anyone who knew him was left better than he found them, especially the adoration temple he built and designed in Saint Joseph Missouri for the Lord. He was not just a war hero, but he was my hero. From his first dance with his wife at a Memorial Day ball, I sure know they are now dancing on streets of gold. Bless you, Poppa and Gwennie. I know you are in the great cloud of witnesses cheering me on. We will make you proud.

5

The Commute

*M*y grandparents changed my life in more ways than one. Now, I had this newfound courage that filled me, and Rebekah and I knew that we **NEEDED** to go to Texas and feel out of the land. We needed to feel the soil, visit, and see what our spirits said as we were there, as we were directed to do by people who had given us wise counsel. It was no longer an "if" we were going to visit but a "when" we would go visit. We had certainty in our spirit that there was something there for us, something we had yet to see. Although we had this bolstering courage to go and see the land, what I also still had was "the commute." There was the courage, and then there was the commute. Throwing myself into that small 2004 Mazda 3 like a sardine in a can season was a devastating one. The reality of my current situation was a constant reminder to me that I would say to myself often, "This is no way to live your life, Jake." I was on the road 6-7 hours a day, working 8-9 hours a day just to hopefully shift it into neutral and recharge my batteries when I got home, but only to be right back in the drive in the blink of an eye to do it all over again. I was not made for this, and every bit of me knew it. Some people can do it, some even love it, and some are called to it, but not this man. Unfortunately, after my wife and I lost everything, this was the process and the waiting season that I was in. Did I pray to the Lord often about this? Oh, wait, I mean, "complain" to the Lord often about this? Yes, I did. I probably annoyed the Lord with the constant "holy" prayers I prayed to Him. "Lord, give me a sign, send me your messenger angels to tell me, give me prophetic word after prophetic word, show me in a dream, tell someone to tell us we need to move to Texas" were also the prayers I would throw up to him ceaselessly.

Even though "brass heavens" were all that I told myself I was hitting for about 11 months, the Lord heard all those prayers … and He did not forget any of them. I remember so clearly one morning as I "complained" (prayed) to Him to change my circumstances. He rebuked me so strongly and said, "Jake, are you done complaining yet? During all this time you've been complaining about your situation, I could be speaking to you about people on your job site!" Have you ever gotten one of those harsh, loving words from your father, mother, or a loved one, and they tell you, "You're so much better than that!"? That's exactly what it felt like on this morning's drive to the Bay Area. This word from the Lord stood me up and demanded my attention when I heard it. Many times, we (myself included) have a hard time receiving correcting words or harsh words because they sting. They're eye-openers; they cut the heart deep, but if heeded and received with an open heart, it can be the very thing that calls us higher and makes us better. After all, Proverbs 27:5 says it like this, "An open rebuke is better than hidden love." Solomon was onto something; there is a reward when a rebuke is stewarded. So rather than the Lord not saying anything, He corrects you. There's an opportunity to be had when we take heed in these moments. The great thing is that He rebukes the ones He loves. So, if that is you who the Lord has rebuked, or maybe it was a parent or a loved one. Remember, it is solely because they love you deeply. To say the least, I was sternly corrected, and in return, I heeded.

Immediately after this occurred, I submitted, humbled myself, and repented to the Lord for my selfish complaining. In this season, I quickly started to realize that the Lord was hearing all of my prayers, but He was testing me. Am I, even in the times when I need something for myself, able to still give to others and be obedient to Him? A true test of character. Did I have the capacity to put aside the complaints about my circumstance and turn them into the breakthrough someone else was praying for? I know many of you who may be reading this today know exactly what I'm talking about, how hard it is to pray for someone else's breakthrough when you are so desperately in need of your own. It just so happened right after I did this, and I repented, after which He spoke to me about a colleague of mine. The Lord spoke to me and said, "Now that I have your attention, there is a man who has two children, and they are both in major trouble." The Lord told me that He wants me to go tell him (my colleague), "I know you've been worried night and day about your children, but rest assured, for I have them in the palm of my hands and that they are going to be restored to the children you once knew."

"Wow, that's a word, Lord," I thought to myself. I knew it was Him who spoke this because my heart started to burn within me, and I suddenly couldn't keep still in my little Mazda 3. The only problem with this, in my opinion, was that I had never talked to this guy one time; I had only seen him passing by or in meetings because he was very high profile. Also, this guy was never alone; for me to tell him something like this, he needed to be alone. Is he even a Christian? Does he even believe the Lord can speak? Is this going to be just way out of left field weird to him? What if he doesn't even have kids? All thoughts running through my head. After thinking and thinking it over again, the feeling that the Lord told me to do this persisted; I couldn't shake it. I NEEDED to obey this leading.

So, I actually got to work a little earlier this day, around 5 A.M., and took a walk down to where this guy's job trailer is, and what do you know, his light was on! Not only that, but he was also in there alone, something that never happens. So, I walked by the trailer and saw that he had a coffee machine in the corner of the door. As a way just to get my foot in the door and have an opportunity to deliver this encouraging word, I knocked on the door to see if I could get some caffeine. I'm definitely a coffee guy. He signaled me in. I asked him if I could "snag a cup of coffee for the early morning really quick." I was just looking for some way to get my foot in the door. "Of course," he said! As the hot water was heating in the machine, we started to talk shop a little bit, and I just introduced myself and told him who I was, what my job was on the job site, and where I was driving from. He replied to me and told me he was the director of this very large division in the company, that he had been with the company for a long time, and that he was a corporate executive. He also said that he has been hearing some amazing things about me from around the company. Right then, as he said that, I thought to myself, "My goodness, this word that the Lord gave me better be right!" Stakes just got higher in my mind. We talked and bantered about sports and life, and a little bit about the city we were working in and how crazy it was with all the restrictions and regulations at that time (Covid was fresh on the scene). I was just about to take my leap of faith and deliver the word, and then his phone rang. He had to take it; it was a pressing call. "It was so great meeting you, and I'll see you around," he stated before he took the call.

So, I walked out of the trailer pretty bummed out because I knew I needed to give him that word. It grieved me that I didn't deliver it and missed my window of time, so I stopped myself in my tracks and turned right back around. I needed to be obedient! I doubled back and V-lined right back to his trailer door with every intent that I was not going to leave that trailer without giving him the word. I popped back into his trailer, and he was still on the phone. He gave me this weird "What are you doing back?" kind of look as if I had forgotten something. Maybe he thought, "Wow, this guy's already back for his second cup of coffee."

I whispered to him, "I'll wait till you are off the call." So, I awkwardly stood there and waited for him to be off the phone so I could tell him the real reason why I stumbled upon his trailer this morning. After what seemed to be the longest 10 minutes of my life awkwardly waiting and nervously tapping my foot, he finally hung up the phone. I could tell he wanted to know what I needed to ask him and that I needed to be quick because he had to go. So I inhaled and just went for it. I said, "Hey man, I wanted to let you know that the real reason I came in this trailer this morning wasn't just for some morning cup of coffee, but it was actually because Jesus loves you, and He wanted me to share a word with you." His eyebrows went up, and he was taken aback as he leaned back in his chair. I continued, "I don't know what you've done, where you've been, or where you're going. I don't even know what you believe in, but I wanted to let you know that I believe that the Lord speaks to me, and many times, He speaks to me on behalf of other people, and this morning, He just so happened to speak to me about you." I told him, "I still believe Jesus works miracles today, I believe He still speaks today, and that He is with us and never forsakes us!"

He replied, "I was raised catholic," and he showed me the rosaries hanging from his computer that he loved so much. So, I spoke strongly and stated to him, "I felt like the Lord put you on my heart because He wanted to let you know that even though you may be worried day and night about your sweet children (I didn't even ask if he had children before I went for it), you have been losing sleep over them, but rest assured, for I the Lord have them in the palm of my hands, and I am going to restore them to the children you once knew."

He started to shed tears. He said that his relationship with his son and his daughter has been so horrible as of late. He nodded his head saying, "Yes, I have kids!" He said his daughter was in a relationship that he strongly disapproved of, and his son won't talk to him about anything at all these days, for he had fallen into a deep depression. He even stated he bought his son a guitar, hoping he would start playing again and maybe kick-start some passion in his life again. He was so blessed by the word, and then he allowed me to lay my hands on him and pray over him and his children. So, I prayed over all of them and asked the Lord for a huge restoration to take place in his family, and I declared that he surely would see the goodness of the Lord in the midst of his family.

After the prayer, he looked at me and said thank you repeatedly. With a refreshed face, he also said to me, "Man, I think it's been at least ten years since someone has prayed for me." What a tragedy, I thought to myself. My heart broke when he said that to me. I thought to myself, how many people are out here right now that have never been prayed for or even know Jesus is merely thinking about them? There are many, and I know there are; maybe it's you reading this today. News flash for you; He's got a billion good thoughts about you, as a matter of fact, more than can outnumber the sands.

"Psalms 139: 17: "How precious also are your thoughts to me, O God! How great is the sum of them! If I should count them, they would be more in number than the sand." Weeks later, after I stewarded this word I received for him, I followed up and asked how things were going with his beloved children and if he had seen any breakthroughs. He said that things have totally shifted with his relationship with his children; his son was connecting with him again, and his daughter confided in him again about her relationship struggles. Look at what the Lord did. He took a morning complainer (me), turned him into a messenger of the Lord, and brought forth a breakthrough to an entire family that desperately needed it! That's what God does!

"The Commute," as you would say, continued forward as you could probably guess, but so did the Lord's mighty hand! As complaining ceased and obedience increased, moments like these encounters continued to occur over and over again as the Lord led me. My morning drives began to become daily intelligence briefs from the Most-High God, where he would give me my marching orders to carry out for the day! Morning drives started to feel like glory drives. My

> "What once was my complaining place became my sustaining place."

whole approach to the season I was in had shifted. All around my workplace, I could share testimony after testimony of what the Lord prevailed to do as I heeded His words. Little did I know that these people I had prayed for would become divinely instrumental in what God had rolled up His sleeve for me. From the rooftop of my project, where people would be healed of leg pain, to the floor level where the Lord used me to speak into an atheist's life. Healings, signs, wonders, and miracles were advancing on my job site.

As crazy as it sounds, the Lord even got an atheist to believe in "the good of this world again" (his words) because I could disagree with him and simply not get mad at him. He had never met a Christian who didn't cuss him out or curse him for simply just disagreeing with him. This young man was in his mid-20s! They all bashed him, tossed him to the side, called him a sinner and deranged beyond repair. Yet none of them ever communicated to him that there was not yet one god, king, prince, or higher power ever mentioned in history, like Jesus himself, who gave up His own life so that you could have yours, so that we can be forgiven for our sins and experience eternal life—the best gift of all, an exchange like none other. Nobody ever told him that there was a God who said, **"I love you so much that I would rather die for you than spend eternity without you."**

After this talk with this individual and many other conversations, he was actually the one who wrote me the most provoking letter of recommendation I had ever seen in my life, which revealed what he really thought about me. Unknown to me throughout our journey, through all the times I took to speak into his life through daily relationships, a couple of words from his recommendation showed me the real impact the Lord made on his life.

In his email, he wrote, "In an environment filled with incompetency and chaos, you are among one of the only people I could count on for anything." This next one blessed me so much; he stated, "Despite our differences, you are a person of exceptional moral character, and you are the living proof of the good there is in humanity." This letter of recommendation revealed to me the Lord's impact on this young man's life. I pray even to this day that those seeds planted in him by the Lord would water and bring into a beautiful fruition into a relationship with Jesus himself, the true living proof of goodness. The Lord used me as an instrument in His hand as I yielded to Him. Throughout this space and time, the Lord was giving me influence, and I was even promoted in my workplace. Although the breakthrough I was looking for had not yet come, the Lord still had plans to pour out his blessing to others, and He had no plans of stopping as I continued to brave the commute and commit myself to this place He had placed me. The time I gave, the hours I spent in that car crying out, praying to the Lord, seeking His voice, and knocking on His door all led me to a culminating point. Thinking He didn't hear my prayers as often as I did, I couldn't have been more wrong. "The commute," as dreadful as it was, served to be the turning point for what He was preparing for me, for what He was about to do in our lives. From the courage my grandpa provoked into me, to the commute where the Lord was maturing me, this all compelled me to a place where the Lord was leading me into "The First Step" that would then change everything we had ever known.

6

The First Step

I jetted home after a long day, burst through the front door, threw myself in a cold shower, grabbed myself some iced coffee (because my wife and I are coffee fanatics), took my wife's hand with my keys in the other, and said, "Let get out of here, it's time to see a sunset." My wife and I craved our alone time in this season as any married couple could probably imagine, but at this moment in our lives, we felt demanded that we retreat, see the Lord's glory, and simply be. Just relax, get away from the chaos, and connect with God and each other. We managed to peel away, find a backroad, and pull off to the shoulder. I rolled the windows down, kicked my foot out the window, and leaned back. My wife and I both connect with the Lord in nature by pondering on the canvas of His creation and the work of His fingertips. It kind of felt like this was the only moment in quite some time that I felt like I could finally take one long, deep breath and exhale from all the craziness of a season we were in. Whenever we intentionally draw back from people and just reset, I always ask myself, "Why don't I do this more often?" I'm sure some of you reading today probably say the same thing to yourself. I mean, throughout the word of God, we find Jesus either peeling away from others, retreating into the garden, or getting away from the crowd so that He could have a direct and undistracted connection with the Father: no chatter, no noise, no echoes, just His father's voice.

He was intentional about that, and every time He did so, He came out filled with strength, vigor, and insight into what His next step was. Healing, signs, wonders, and miracles also flowed out of that place as a result. Doing this with just my wife and me to receive some fresh wind of perspective was vital. We could feel the weight and anticipation for what we knew we had to do but didn't quite know how it was going to happen or unfold in our lives, but we felt the weight of the air of expectation. I remember reading a quote that rocked me and offered me great insight into taking steps with the Lord. It went like this by Frederick Douglas: I prayed for 20 years but received no answer until I prayed with my legs. Boom, that one struck me to the core. It's essentially saying that prayers without ACTION do not

> "I prayed for 20 years but received no answer until I prayed with my legs."
> *Frederick Douglas*

come to fruition. It might be true to say that some of us are waiting and praying on God to do something like He's the one stuck when, in reality, He's waiting on YOU to DO something in FAITH! Remember from the "In the Waiting" chapter that the Lord is waiting on you to see what you do while you're waiting on Him. He's looking to see what your response is. I then thought to myself, of all the people in my life that I knew were just stuck in the same place, waiting and waiting and waiting for God to do something for them … but when you come back or talk to them years later, they're smack dab still in the same place more stuck than stuck can be. What a shame it would be to live the same year out 75 times and then call it a life. Sadly, many people do that and do not know that there's more to be had. They simply can't even see that they are selling themselves short! "God will do it when He's ready; I'm just in a desert season", is something they say often.

If God really wanted it, He would just do it for me. Not everybody can do what that person does (talking about someone living their life to the fullest potential); these are some of the words that proceed from the mouths of individuals like this; faithless words. All the faith needs to be carried by the Lord, and none of the faith has to be carried by them; responsibility is a long-lost friend to them. I love in the Bible when the Lord calls out to Abraham and tells him to depart from his father's house and go to a land he does not know, but a land that He will show him. The Lord is making a promise to him about the blessed inheritance He wanted to pioneer through Abraham. Abraham takes the Lord up on His word, obeys, believes, and does it! First, he had the faith to believe it, and then he had the legs that physically moved him into the place God was going to show him. What does that tell us? Read that one again. Not only did Abraham immediately obey the Lord, but he also BELIEVED the Lord in

> **Faith carried on the legs of obedience changes the course of history.**

what He said He would do. If you're not familiar with this moment in history, Genesis 12:1 tells it best when the Lord is speaking to Abraham and says, *"Get out of your country, from your family, and from your father's house, to a land that I will show you. I will make you a great nation; I will bless you and make your name great; and you shall be a blessing. I will bless those who bless you, and I will curse him who curses you; and in you all the families of the earth shall be blessed".* So the Lord drops this on Abraham, and three chapters later in Genesis 15 states, "Then He brought him outside and said, *"Look now toward heaven, and count the stars if you are able to number them." And He said to him, "So shall your descendants be." And Abraham Believed the Lord, and He accounted it to him for righteousness."* Abraham believed what the Lord told him, and the Lord delighted in that. How many times do we doubt the things the Lord has spoken over our lives and not believe Him? We think He was either wrong when He said it to us, or He may have misspoken.

Where it takes us ten years to finally come into alignment with what God initially spoke over us, what if we could believe Him right at once when He says it? Abraham believed the Lord

Delayed obedience is disobedience.

not only with his heart but also with his feet; he moved them and showed the Lord evidence of his faith. In order for the Lord's promise to be made manifest in Abraham's inheritance, key ingredients of faith (evidence of things hoped for yet not seen), belief (trusting and taking the Lord at His word), and action (the evidence of trusting in Him) had to be in the mix. I'd like to propose to anyone reading this book at this moment that the same ingredients apply to all of us no matter what walk of life you are in right now. Now, I'm not saying my sweet Rebekah and I were about to be a modern-day Abraham and Sarah within this new compelling journey the Lord was leading us into, but we knew we had to DO something (though it is kind of funny that our names are Rebekah and Jacob; children of Abraham in the Bible). It is kind of like when the Lord told Abraham not where to go, but He said, "Leave and go to a land I will show you." In like manner, we knew that the Lord was going to show us when we got there.

As my leg hung out the window and we took in the sunset on that lovely evening, I had an epiphany. As my eyes looked all the way down the road that eventually led right into the horizon line of the sunset, I could see the whole course, the whole picture. Yes indeed, it was a beautiful California sunset. At that very moment, I recalled a Bible verse that had been engraved into my life ever since I was a kid: *Proverbs 16:9, "A man plans His course, but the Lord determines his steps."* As I continued to gaze and place my eyes on the plain of the road that led all the way across the city right into the sunset, I felt the Lord gently nudge my spirit and say to me, "You see, son, I see that you want to plan and understand the whole course in front of you, but right now all I'm asking of is **your first step**. I'm going to determine where you end up." I knew right then that taking the first step would be the curtain that peeled back the next one! It was time to carry faith on the legs of obedience. I felt Him speak this to my spirit so strong it was like I got hit with a fresh revelation. I knew it was Him, and I knew what I needed to do. It provoked life into me. Funny enough, this was a verse I've known my whole life that has now actually jumped off of the pages and into my spirit. I knew this was from the Lord because this verse came out of nowhere; I wasn't thinking of it, and it wasn't something I read in my daily encounter that morning; no, this was spontaneously inspired upon me by the spirit and divinely brought forward by the Lord.

The human condition says, "I need to know how everything is going to happen before it happens." On the contrary, the faith condition says, "Even though I don't know how anything is going to unfold, I simply trust You because You said it!" We walk by faith and not by sight, and it is impossible to please the Lord without it (faith). If He said it to you, you can trust that He's going to prove it to you. Something had to have been in that caffeine that night. I turned to Rebekah and shared with her what had just hit me, and her spirit in the same leaped and resonated with every bit of it; she was ready to take that first step. I might even say she was ready before I ever was. She was closely in touch with a spirit of courage in this season. From the girl I knew I sat next to in the 5th grade to the girlfriend I received in October of 2018 to the wife I now have, she had grown leaps and bounds beyond what I ever expected. She often provoked life into me and directed me to set my faith and dream dreams that scared me. She continually compelled me to think bigger than what my mind had ever dared to conceive. A mighty man of God once said to me: If your dreams do not scare you when you look at them, you must dream way bigger. Needless to say, this dream was very scary to us, but being

> "If your dreams do not scare you when you look at them, you must dream way bigger."

scared isn't a sign to stop going forward. It is a sign that courage is going to be needed.

The Lord knew what He was doing as we connected with Him that beautiful evening. He stirred us up and put fire under our feet. What do you know? We peeled away, removed ourselves from distraction, and connected with God through nature, and He spoke, just like Jesus modeled for us. I encourage everyone who feels weighed down and burdened by the pressures and distractions of the world to do this very thing. Break away, get to that space that only you would know that brings you peace, and simply just breathe in the presence of God. Connect with Him, and make room for Him to speak. Maybe you bring your significant other with you, and you both do it. Is it at a coffee shop? Is it early in the morning before the sun rises, and you go for a run? Is it in the presence of worship as you align your heart with Him? Do you connect with Him by turning off the lights, lighting some candles, and seeking Him in solitude? Is it at night when all your children finally have made it to bed? Is it in your designated prayer closet, where you close the door and shut out all the outside noise with it? Is it in nature where you gaze upon His handiwork and catch the wind of His breath? Where is it? Ask yourself. If you don't know where it is, pray to the Lord to show you. Get to that still place and just say, "Speak, Lord; your servant is listening." Just watch what He does; He surely is a rewarder to those who diligently seek Him, and I can personally vouch for Him; He gives good gifts.

After that night, Rebekah and I felt like we had caught a strong wind of refreshing. It was time. We told my parents that we would fly out to Texas, scout out some land, and see what the Lord speaks to us. Nothing of a surprise to them … They and my family have been hearing all about Texas from us for months now. We were planning to book the flight and also made a map of all the places we would go from South to Central Texas. Up to this point of the journey, we still hadn't gotten any kind of prophetic word from anyone we were asking from, and we also had not had anyone come to us and say they had a dream and the Lord showed them that we were to move.

As previously mentioned in prior chapters, the counsel we received also encouraged us to be very practical up to this point. Despite all that, we knew that we were being led by Him above all else, and He would show us otherwise. This became a maturing place for Rebekah and me because it wasn't a word from someone else we were running on but a word from the Lord Himself that we knew we had to obey. This directly means that all of our trust will be placed in Him only, and not what man or woman has said to us. Exactly where He wants us; all that is required of us is to hear God and obey God. That's what we set out to do. After speaking to my parents about us getting our flight ready to go to Texas, my mom and dad both said they wanted to go, too! They insisted on going and experiencing it with us, and it didn't really seem like they'd accept no for an answer! A first step was needed, so a first step was taken; this was just the beginning of all that we could have never known. Right now, as I type this, I can actually feel the anticipation rising up again as I relive all that the Lord did.

*(**Testimony Note**): Today, up to this point in the book where you are reading, it is September 30th of the year 2022 in my life. At the beginning of this story, I mentioned to you that I started typing this on March 20th of the year 2022. If you do the math, a little under six months have passed since I started putting my fingers on this keyboard in my office here in Godley, Texas. There has been a shout to the rooftop miracle that has just taken place for Rebekah and me! The river in the desert has burst through like a roaring glacier! The wasteland has become a dreamland. The very cry of our hearts we have cried out for all of our lives apart, and all of our lives together is coming. The mountain that stood in front of us has now been made low. WE ARE PREGNANT with our first beloved child! Yes, it has happened! When I began to write this story and dedicated this story to our children, I had hoped one day all of you (the readers reading) and them (my inheritance) would see through this story, and the timeline of His faithfulness promise come to life. He has done it! What seemed impossible is now on its way to the earth. As for the readers who are reading: There's nothing impossible for our God! As for our children reading one day: I want you to know September 30th of 2022 is now one of the best days of your Mom and I's entire life. Lord, our cry back to you as you have answered our prayer is that*

"They will never be ours, and they will always be yours." We give this child and all the ones you choose to entrust us with right back to you!)

7

Treasure Hunt

*T*he flight was booked, the rental car was ready, and the bags packed. All the while, we were not telling anyone what we were doing or where we were going at the time. Rebekah and I wanted this trip to be something we took without any noise surrounding it or any opinions or assumptions that might arise from it. We knew this whole thing was a bit crazy, and a lot of people wouldn't understand it. We decided that if the Lord did want to use somebody to speak into this faith-taking adventure we were embarking on, we knew He would, and it would be real and raw without people knowing we were even visiting Texas. Our hearts' quest was simply that we were just to "GO." Nothing more and nothing less.

There was no firm destination of where we were scoping out to be. However, I put together a little map of the route we would take through the heart of Texas, starting from the airport where we landed. Even so, it felt just exactly like my dad had told me; "Jake, this feels exactly like a treasure hunt," he said to me! It felt kind of like when I was a kid, and around easter time every year, the family and I would do a treasure hunt. Where my dad would come to rally the troops in the house and tell everyone, "Ok, get ready, kids, it's time for a treasure hunt. Let's go find some treasure," and then you, not knowing where the hunt was, would be led by your father into the general vicinity of where all the "treasure hunting" was about to happen. The easter eggs would be stuffed with money, candy, little army man toys, and other shenanigans that would make us all go crazy. Some of you may have had a similar experience with your family during this time of the year. This was the same, yet just a little twist. This treasure hunt we were embarking on wasn't my earthly father who was leading me into where the treasure was; it was my heavenly father that we were trusting to lead us right where He wanted us to be. It was a little scary, a little fun, and, for the most part, pretty crazy, and we knew that it was. I remember some of the family that we had told about the trip humbly would ask, "So where are you guys going to go?" and we would just reply, "We have no idea"! And that's because we truly didn't. We felt like there was a door we were being led to. However, we had no clue what would be on the other side if and when we opened it. We did know that faith would open the door, and the rest was up to the Lord.

So, the day had come; my wife, mom, dad, and I were getting ready to head out the door en route to the airport. We gathered around and decided to start our trip by praying together. We prayed and intentionally acknowledged the Lord to give God the driver's seat for this entire trip. We prayed together, acknowledged Him, and asked that the Lord "lead us in His way and His truth throughout the whole trip and help us to find your treasure." We asked the Lord to put His fingerprints on this trip in whatever way He wanted to. The prayer ended. We were getting ready to walk out the door, and then our house-sitting family friends had just arrived to keep watch over the territory for the time being; they were truly amazing people. I remember this moment, for it was an important word that Rebekah and I would cling to later down the road. She had grabbed Rebekah and me very urgently and, with a voice of urgency, stated, "I really feel like the Lord wanted me to tell you something. She had

You will know when you land!"

to tell us that she wouldn't let us leave without knowing that which was placed on her heart. I can recall Rebekah and I looking at each other after that and now being completely consumed with utter anticipation for our landing. Up to this point, that was really the only directing and guiding word we had received pertaining to the start of our journey. And so it began …

Throughout this journey, we asked the Lord to open supernatural doors for us. We had declared Isaiah 22:22 over the entire trip! Isaiah 22:22 declares, *"I will place on his shoulder the key to the house of David; what he opens no one can shut, and what he shuts no one can open."* This verse has been a staple for Rebekah and me throughout our entire union. This verse states that the Lord is our doorkeeper and gatekeeper and that other people can't keep us off the destiny the Lord has for us. It shouts that obstacles and hurdles cannot keep you from what God ordained for you. If He opens the doors, no man can shut it, and no man can deter it from happening. This was our proclamation: that he would open doors no man can shut and close doors that no man could open in this season.

Funny enough, right from the get-go, this started to become evident. We sat in Row 2, Seats 22 and 23. If you don't think that the Lord still speaks through numbers, you may have a different perspective by the end of this story. We sat down in our seats, noting that we were already seeing evidence of what we had prayed for with our Isaiah 22:22 declaration. And so there we were, I specifically in the tight as tight can be Boeing 737 Max, cramming my legs to the ceiling (per usual in airplanes for me) and ready for take-off. It doesn't matter where I'm going on a plane; I usually spend the entirety of my time anytime I'm on a plane praying, worshipping, and seeking the Lord. I sometimes feel like I connect with the Lord better when on a plane (maybe because I'm closer to heaven). I was praying and continuing to speak life over the trip, and just like that, before I knew it, we were already landing in Austin, TX! I guess the flight was about 3 hours and 30 minutes, but that sure wasn't what I felt.

Because of the word that we had received from our family friend before we left on our flight that "We would know when we landed," Rebekah and I had built up quite an anticipation for the plane's landing. I remember unbuckling our seat belts and looking at each other with our lips sealed and our eyebrows all the way up, both of us wondering if either of us had felt something. With hopeful eyes, I asked her if she felt anything, and she responded, "No, I don't feel anything." She returned the question, and I laughingly stated, "No, I don't feel anything other than this crazy thick humidity!" We both laughed at each other because this humidity straight-up slapped us in our faces as if we were only just making our way off the plane and onto the terminal! Everyone in the Midwest knows exactly what I mean. With thick sweat running down our faces in the air, we felt like we were swimming through. We got all our bags and finally found our rental car. So the journey began, and we moved up the heart of Texas from the South to the North. No plan, no destination, no reservations anywhere, just moving by faith. I did, however, draft up a little printed-off map of Texas with us landing in Austin and traveling our way up to Dallas throughout the week. It was December, and everywhere we went was decorated for Christmas. It didn't matter if we were at the Austin, Texas

State Capitol dancing by the big Christmas tree, rolling through old town Georgetown admiring the old architecture, making our way through historic Waco looking at the Silos, J-walking through the skyscrapers of Dallas, moving along the brick roads of Fort Worth, or just passing by places we had no clue about; we continued to see something.

As we drove to different areas around the state, a common theme that we continued to see was the "22" numbers and the word "joy." It didn't matter where we went or what we were doing; whether it was a restaurant, a gas station with the price of $2.22 if it was a billboard we were driving by, our air B&B confirmation number, our boarding passes, rental car license plate number, a poster we were walking by, the hotel room number we were staying in, or the model home we walked through; we continued to see the "22" number or a phrase that included "joy" or just the word "joy" itself. It followed us, and it amazed us over and over again every time we stumbled into it. In addition, this wasn't something I was just witnessing or experiencing; rather, this was a whole group revelation that my mom, dad, wife, and I were all seeing. This wasn't just happenstance or just a coincidence; I don't believe it was a coincidence. It was undeniable to ignore and impossible not to acknowledge. It's kind of funny that before we left on the trip, we were declaring Isaiah 22:22 (Keys of David), and crazy enough, this was the very number we were seeing be made known time and time again. No, we were not "manifesting" this on our own ability by the law of attraction; rather, the Lord divinely ordered our steps by His ability and sovereign hand. Each and every time Rebekah and I saw this number, we would intentionally remind ourselves of our declaration over the trip and intentionally pray for doors to fling wide open for us. When we saw the word "joy" meeting us wherever we went, we would then partner with what we felt the Holy Spirit was speaking and pray, "Lord, pour out your **unspeakable joy** upon us, and let the **joy** of the Lord be our strength." One very eye-opening part of the word "joy" that we were seeing was that it seemed to be an exact contrary declaration to the season we were currently walking through. Better yet, it was the polar opposite. That's often how prophecy works; it is an opposite declaration of the season you are fighting through. Where the spirit clashes with the flesh and declares the truth. At the sight of these common occurrences, we began to continually prophesy "open doors" and "joy." I know I shined a light on several instances of the tragedy and agony my family was walking through in prior chapters; nonetheless, this word "joy" seemed to be refreshingly arriving just on time.

From walking heel deep in heartbreak and tragedy at this time in our life, I know some of you can attest to the fact that when it rains, it pours … and man, it was pouring. I remember sometimes, in certain moments, just helplessly throwing my hands in the air while bad news continued to pour down on us and just saying, "What else can possibly happen?" We were completely at a lack of control over anything happening to us and around us in this season of life. By far the most crushing of a season I've come to face with. Just to quickly expound: From being wrongly accused while in a multi-million-dollar business with my father, to a worldwide pandemic wreaking havoc all around, to my wife and I losing our jobs and first apartment together, to losing my Grandma Gwennie, then to losing my grandpa shortly after, and then my beloved cousin gone too soon at the age of 28. This isn't me just trying to initiate some woe-is-me sop story; no, this is me being honest with you that even as a strong man and leader in my life, this season was breaking me, then breaking me, and then breaking me again. To say the least, and to tell you the truth, this was by far the worst season of brokenness I had ever experienced. Many times, I'd find myself having an average day, and then, at the drop of a pin, I'd be weeping and struggling in grief for hours. This went on for a while, but joy was on the way.

Faith was rising. We knew that something was birthed in the spirit but was not yet seen in the physical. He was making this evident. The Lord was still moving on our behalf. All the while, we couldn't see it. Psalms 126: 6 encourages me in saying,

> "Those who sow with tears, will reap with songs of joy."
> *Psalms 126:6*

"Those who sow with tears, will reap with songs of joy. He

who continually goes forth weeping, bearing seed for sowing, shall doubtless come again with rejoicing, bringing his sheaves with him." We were definitely full-fledge forward in the "sow with tears" season and were eagerly anticipating the "songs of joy" season. This is a promise, and we were sure of it. We were seeing the beginning works of this starting to come forth. Time went on, and we journeyed from City to City and place to place. Just like we had been seeing, we experienced profound joy. We were enjoying every moment of our time. Our joint laughter was unlimited; we were smiling from ear to ear on all of our car rides, and even in the midst of all we had gone through, the Lord was blessing and refreshing us. You may be asking, "How could you be so joyful even when you were all experiencing such great pain?" My answer would be, "I don't know, but because I was doing it **with** Him, it was easy in His presence." There is no logical answer to that question because it was all supernatural; it wouldn't make sense to the mind. There was actually a day when we went to a specific lake in the Austin area, where my father and I felt struck to rally our wives together to intercede and pray for His favor and continued direction in this trip. We felt the urge to intercede and pray over this ordained time together as well as ask the Father for new revelations for our family legacy with the recent loss we were walking through. I remember it so clearly.

This specific day, it was actually an overcast afternoon with a slight forecast of rain and not much sunshine on the radar. As we were praying and simply just thanking Him for His goodness, the sky literally had parted, countless clouds moved out of the way, and without a ray of sunshine present anywhere else, the sun shined directly upon us and the bench we were praying on. It was almost as if a heavenly strobe light was put on us. Nobody was out on the water, nobody was in the parking lot area, nobody was near the lake's sandbar; it was just me, my family, and the straight glory of the Lord shining on us. All in one private, intimate moment. It was nothing short of spectacular as we just sat there, filled with the pure awe and wonder of what had just taken place. We knew the Lord was listening to us pray that day, just as we knew He was the entire time. As for me, I know after that day, I was feeling a tug of war in the deep depths of my heart. I had known the depths of grief I was in this season. However, at the same time, I also felt pregnant with the feeling and knowing that God was birthing something new in me. One part of me was losing all I had ever known, and the other part of me felt like new seeds were breaking forth through the soils of my heart. One part of me was suddenly dying, and another part of me was slowly coming to life. Now that I ponder and look back, it makes me think of John 12:24, which states, "*Truly, truly, I say to you, unless a grain of wheat falls into the earth and dies, it remains alone; but if it dies, it bears much fruit.*" Even with the sorrows that came with a loved one's passing on, I felt the rumblings of new life starting to break ground.

I know I mentioned in Chapter 4 how one of the final talks with my Grandpa gave me a new courage and faith in the impossible; well, this was similar to that. With the passing, specifically with my grandma, I felt like there was another transfer of courage that came over me. Another measure of it. Something had to fall and die (like the grain of wheat) for new life to make its debut. On one cheek rolled down tears of sorrow, but then tears of joy flowed down the other—a mix of feelings and emotions I had never simultaneously felt in my life until now. I guess you could have called me a "beautiful mess" at this time, but it was only because God was doing deep work inside of me. Some days, the only way to put it is that it felt like I was going through heart surgery. He was healing places of pain and agony while striking cords of destiny that were always there. It's a truly fascinating dichotomy all tied together. I know I'll never forget this time of my life, even as this story ages.

The journey carried on from that day, for that day was just a precursor to the more God had in store. We continued from place to place and City to City as the Lord continued to pour out His doses of refreshing joy upon us. Moving from one location to another, there came a night when we all wanted to visit a church and pray together. We were in Waco at the time, and the church we sought was all the way in the Dallas-Fort Worth Metroplex. It was dumping rain on this day, I mean dumping. The rain wasn't falling vertically; it was flying horizontally. Any past Californians reading this know that we were taught and shown that rain only falls vertically and no other way. Well, that certainly wasn't the case on this Texas night! Nonetheless, we still strongly felt we were supposed to attend this church. We braved the storm, with windshield wipers flying 100 miles per hour left to right. We made it to the church after an hour and a half later. One of the senior lead pastors was speaking that night. My wife and I were filled with the expectation that the Lord would give us clarity. After all, we were here in Texas, and what better time than the Lord to speak to us while we were here? We arrived at the church and were very eager to get out of the storm and into the building. We finally sat down, and the service was great. At one point during this pastor's message, he said something that literally made Rebekah and I look at each other wide-eyed and shaken. He stated word for word (as it seemed like he was looking directly at us), "This is the season to double down on your risky faith; it's time to double down on your risky faith." Our spirits latched onto that word as it resonated with us completely. A combination of more twos and also the firm reminder this was the season to take risks! He also mentioned and taught out of the verse, and I couldn't believe it when he said it, Isaiah 22:22, which blew our mind.

> **"It's time to double down on your risky faith."**

The keys of David. The very verse that we had been partnering with for the whole season that we were in. He stated that as we began to step into risky faith, the open doors would fling wide open. This was by no chance a coincidence. No, it wasn't; this was perfectly aligned with His voice. God deposited another dose of fresh faith and courage right into the spirit of my wife and I. This wasn't too good to be true, this was true because He is good! The Lord knew we would be there on this night. My mom and dad also looked at me right when it was said with a look that displayed, "That was for you …" Nothing else from that night stuck with us other than that which was just said. We couldn't stop thinking about it. It wasn't that what He said was so profound. It was that just what he said literally was inspired by the Holy Spirit and hit us so powerfully in conjunction with what we were contending for. It actually kind of scared me to hear him say that because I felt like it was further pushing me to do the unthinkable. I know Rebekah felt the same after conversing with her. The church service was over, and Texas hospitality was alive and active. Everyone we met was so nice and so respectful beyond measure. It was a blessing. We headed back home that night very late. However, every bit of the drive was worth it, for we knew the Lord used this night to bolster our courage and confirm to us that we were on the right track in this wonderful "treasure hunt" of ours.

Hours turned into days, and days quickly turned into the ten full days of a complete time, which would cap off our trip. So much had taken place, and so much joy had been experienced that before we knew it, it was time to head back to the West Coast. This faith-taking trip was every bit of the words a "treasure hunt." I didn't even get to capture all of it in this chapter, for there was even more that took place beyond what was mentioned. From divine appointments to the glory shining on us out at the lake in Austin, to the rainy night church service, from house tours and City tours to praying for a woman's back inside of a house showing and her being instantaneously healed, to endless confirmations of His joy, to the number 22 meeting us at our every turn, and cups of refreshing waters quenching our spirits. We arrived with sorrow, but we left with joy, and I'm not just speaking for myself. At the end of the day, Rebekah and I felt like we had responded to the Lord in obedience. He told us to "go and see," and we did that. The rest of our riveting story was going to take some crazy faith.

8

Crazy Faith

We came, we saw, and best of all, we were obedient. This sweet adventure of ours had to come to an end, but at the same time, you could say it was just beginning. My family and I were en route back to the West Coast and getting ready to land back in the Bay Area. My wife and I sat next to each other the whole flight home, for all we could do was sit and ponder all that the Lord had done in our lives on this trip. With our hearts still at a tear between what we felt the Lord was leading us to, we now knew all that we used to only talk about in real life. The picture had now come to real life for us. The flight was about to touch down on the landing strip as we prepared to brace ourselves. A smooth landing quickly came, and we were rounding about the terminal to get ready to disembark. When we landed and the plane came to a complete halt, something interesting happened. My wife grabbed my arm, and with eyes of both urgency and sadness, she looked at me and said, "My heart hurts, I'm homesick!" She was instantly overcome with pure emotion and sadness on that plane in just an instant. Actual tears were welling up in her eyes. She truly looked like she was homesick. The odd thing was we just landed home. She wasn't homesick because she

"My heart hurts, I'm homesick!"

missed where we were returning to; she was homesick from the heart of Texas, which we just left. I thought her choice of word of use in saying "homesick" was perfectly communicated from the spirit. "Homesick" indicates the word "home" in it, which therein lies that she knew she wanted a "home" there.

She wanted a life there; she could see it, and she could just about taste it. Instantly after, she said that I had an epiphany and remembered our family friend who was watching my parents' house while we were gone, and she said with urgency right before we left, "You'll know when you land!" "How crazy is that?" I thought to myself. I got goosebumps; it dawned on me … It was all flip-flops about how we thought and envisioned that word unfolding for us. We thought that word was meant for when we arrived in Texas, but no, it was directly meant for when we landed back home while leaving it behind us. I remember relaying it to my wife, and just as I was communicating it to her, tears started flowing from her eyes. In agreement, we both believed that that specific word given to us was exactly spoken for this moment. The dots were connecting, and things were all starting to line up! Yes, indeed, we were homesick. I think at this point, just between Rebekah and I, in our hearts and spirits, we knew that it wasn't a matter of "if" we were going to be making this crazy move, but it was "when" we were going to do it. The Lord was already starting to grow our wings and preparing us to take flight. We were moving into a take-off position.

If everything that transpired on the trip, alongside being "homesick" upon our landing, wasn't enough to prime the pump of our faith, buckle up. We made it home silently that night and got to unpacking our bags and getting ready to jump right back into our normal, mundane routine work week. Can I just say how hard it was to get ready to go right back into the normal routine of things after experiencing something like we just did? It was painful. The next day, and I'm telling you exactly the next day after we landed, Rebekah received a text. This text came from a family member whom we love dearly; one who we know speaks to the Lord, hears from Him, and walks in a daily relationship with Him. Keep in mind that we did not tell one soul about our trip to Texas beforehand or even after the fact with what we had experienced. The few people we told didn't even know we had made it back to California from our trip yet. I wanted to provide that disclaimer because it only further strengthens the magnitude of what the Lord was about to say. She knew nothing of our whereabouts and certainly knew not of what the Lord had been doing in us for months. Here comes a dose of crazy faith. The text read, ***"Ok, girl,*** *you're in my heart. There is a Spirit air of expectation. Be ready to move when He says move. Do not hesitate or measure. Take the step He lays before you and your Jake. Step out boldly, not looking to the left or to the right, and not looking backwards. The Lord will steady you. The Lord will open doors and close doors. No man will be able to gauge the situation or circumstance because He will be the One doing it. He is giving you faith for this season."* A clear word from the Lord had been delivered, which shook our core. Literally, the day after we landed back home, the Lord delivered unto us a message of guidance, encouragement, and boldness. Just the fuel we needed to prepare our spiritual engine. As if that wasn't enough, she went on to state that the Lord also revealed a picture to her a week ago. I thought to myself, "A week ago would have been perfectly in cadence with the time that we were in Texas." When she says that the "Lord revealed a picture" to her, it means that the Lord uses pictures in her spirit to speak, reveal, and communicate with her. It's a way that she connects with God, and then the Lord inspires and breathes upon it like a spiritual daydream. In what would leave my jaw on the ground, the text went on to state, *"I saw a picture about a week ago. I had just laid down for the night, and I saw the word JOY rising up out of the ground in large letters with flowers and plants all around. The word God has given you and Jake is JOY. It does not stop there. He is giving you a Joy Garden. You will be planting and reaping in joy this year. Your Joy harvest will be bountiful and abundant. It will be beautiful and fragrant."* "Are you kidding me?" I thought to myself. The word "JOY" was at it again; the word that we constantly saw at our every blink while we were in Texas. All the while, we were seeing joy all around us in Texas, and the Lord was showing her the Joy that was to be all around us. It was divine alignment. Now, let's take some inventory. So, the word, "You'll know when you land," had come to pass; Rebekah became "homesick" upon arrival. The spontaneous word from our family member to "be ready to move when he says move … the Lord will open doors and close doors," aligned with the rhythm of our spirits of Isaiah 22:22 for the declaration of our season. Then the exclamation point of a prophetic word that the Lord was "giving us the word joy, and giving us a JOY garden" capped it off.

All the things we were praying, all the things we were asking for, all the things we were declaring, the Lord in His way and divine timing delivered. The beautiful part of it all was that the Lord confirmed it to us just one day after returning home from the trip. Rebekah and I couldn't believe it, for the Lord was surely on the move behind the scenes, already speaking to people and working things out on our behalf. The Great Orchestrator, you could say. All I could do was think back to all the moments when I prayed (complained) to the Lord but felt like I was hitting brass and steel heavens. I couldn't have been more wrong; as a matter of fact, I was the furthest thing from correct. Instead of striking brass heavens, I was actually striking the heart of a loving and attentive Father—one who wanted to answer me just as badly as I wanted Him to move into our life.

He wasn't stuck, nor were my prayers; it was all laid out for me by Him in accordance with His perfect timing. He knew everything down to the detail of how it would transpire, how it would work out, and the way in which it would unfold. Remember, He's not the one stuck. Many times, it's our obedience. In hindsight, looking back now, after Rebekah and I were **obedient** to "Go and see," which the Lord told us, the floodgates of the confirmations and miracles we'd been praying for began to open! This was just the start of this miracle flow. It seemed like it was a trigger point for the Lord. Once we stopped going around the merry-go-round of questions and doubts and actually put our boots on the ground, it all shifted. It was all after the fact. Obedience was a precursor to the miracles He had in store for us. The Lord always rewards obedience, and obedience always produces fruit. That's why it's impossible to please the Lord without faith. Faith is designed to be carried on the legs of obedience. I could feel His pleasure over us. She was right, "He's giving us faith for this season." Might I say crazy faith?

> Once He saw our faith move, we saw His hand move.

What is crazy faith? Crazy faith is only crazy faith if you show yourself "crazy" enough to "do" what He leads you to do. Still though, what even is it? I thought long and hard about what this chapter really means to me, for it can be defined in so many different facets and described in so many different ways by various people. Let's first define faith for what it actually is. "Faith" is the substance of things hoped for, the evidence of things not yet seen (Hebrews 11:1). I can't see it yet, I can't feel it yet, I don't know when it's coming, but the hope inside of us knows the promise will be delivered by the one and only Deliverer; now that's faith.

To me, crazy faith is where faith as a concept is nothing, but faith as an action is everything, where talking about it leaves you bankrupt, and being about it becomes paramount. The

Faith as a concept is nothing, but faith as an action is everything"

writer of Ecclesiastes 5:3 spins it like this, "For a dream comes through much activity, and a fool's voice is known by his many words." Read that Bible verse every morning before your day, and I guarantee you will be more productive! This verse declares that dreams come through "activity," and foolishness is rendered through idle blabbing. Crazy faith is where you throw out all of the books you've read about faith, set aside all the self-help articles you've come across, stop diagnosing how faith turned out for someone else, and stare at the reflection of yourself and make a deal that you are now going to **DO** the very thing He told you to. It's as if you found yourself sitting at a Barnes and Noble reading about everyone else's story your whole life while forgetting to ever pen your own.

Meanwhile, down the road of this crazy faith of ours, there was still something else. All the practical things that continued to knock on my door and request to enter. Exactly just like the questions I mentioned in previous chapters: "Are you seriously considering taking a daunting jump like this? What family do I even have out there? Do I even have one friend who remotely lives in the state? What am I going to do there for work? Is it really worth leaving all of my family behind to pursue this pipe dream? Is there a community there for me? What sense does it make to leave a 6-figure job? How are we even going to find a place to stay? You and your wife are trying to start your family. Do you really not want to have insurance? Is the weather really as excruciating as everyone keeps trying to scare me about? Did God really say and lead us here? How am I going to lead my wife into the complete unknown and be strong? These were just a fraction of the questions that barged at my door. It seemed like the closer we got in the spirit to the Lord leading us here, the more resistance and questions in the practical that pestered my mind day in and day out. Even though these questions knocked, I did acknowledge them and chose not to answer the door. Why? Well, it's simple: I trusted Him. I was way over my head; a perfect place to be when I fully rely on Him to do the heavy lifting.

Crazy faith is where you dare to jump off the billboard and grow your wings on the way down, trusting that the air of His spirit will bear you up. It was about to be that time, the time to mount up on wings like Eagles.

9

Grow Your Wings

*I*t had been about a week or so since we had been back from the trip. As mentioned, the Lord was showing up in ways I couldn't even describe, and He wasn't showing any signs of stopping yet. Many times, all that would be left for me to say was, "Wow, God" while trying to reach down and pick my jaw up from the ground. Still not knowing exactly how everything was going to unravel for us, even though He was clearly speaking, I was quickly back on the grind, back on the road, and right back to Chapter 5, "The Commute." It seemed like the longer that we took to make our decision to finally make the move, the more convicted I started to feel week by week that passed by. After weeks had gone by, Rebekah brought it up one day and urgently felt like we needed to start getting boxes and packing our stuff. I thought to myself, "We don't even know when we are leaving, the timing of it all, and if it will even be this year?" –These were logical thoughts in my head that opposed her request. She insisted that this was a "prophetic act of faith" we needed to take and do in now. By getting boxes and packing our stuff, we would be prophetically declaring to the Lord that we were ready to move when He says so and that we believe in this just as much as He is showing us. The prophetic word we had received said, "Be ready to move and do not hesitate." That's exactly what we were readying ourselves for.

> **You don't have to get ready if you stay ready.**

We wanted to partner with that prophetic word and show the Lord we were intentional in trusting Him and what He said. Not knowing when we would be moving, not knowing what area we would be going to, not knowing what jobs we would have; there we were, two crazy people, carrying bundles of boxes up and down the stairs of my parent's house while trying to act sly—a prophetic act of faith. Knowing we looked weird in the natural, we knew that we were declaring something more profound in the supernatural. I like this quote from Pastor Russell Johnson of Pursuit Northwest in Seattle, who says, "Prophecy isn't a guarantee. It's an invitation to intentional obedience." You choose what to do with it. We were choosing to meet the Lord with our faith as he met us with His voice. We were declaring in the supernatural that this door would open and that the Lord would make a way where there was none. We were responding to his word, and we were going to treat it like it was already done.

This was crazy faith. The substance of things hoped for, yet not seen. We weren't telling anyone that we were packing our stuff and getting ready; we didn't want to freak out our families all the while, and we didn't even know how to explain what was happening. I remember one day, Rebekah and I had gotten some boxes from a friend and were unloading them from Rebekah's car. I was carrying quite a load of them, trying to smuggle them in with one hand while struggling to open the door with my other. Unknown to my parents that we were getting boxes and packing our stuff, my mom opened the door to her amazement of me drowning in boxes. My mother is a very prophetic person. She always has been, so I knew she would understand what we were doing. However, I was still her baby boy. She opened the door and said, "What are you doing? Are you moving?" As she scrambled to help me grab the toppling boxes. I replied, "Yes, we will be moving," in the most gentle and sincere tone I could respond with. She was wide-eyed and confused and didn't quite understand what I was communicating, but then I could see it finally registering in her mind. It dawned on her that the reality of this was literally at her front door. It was almost as if a very sudden sadness had come upon her, for she now knew that this was not just some talk or fantasy, but rather this was the reality of what was about to be, and now we were preparing for it. She understood what we were doing, and something in her understood that it was going to happen soon. That's what I interpreted from the changing countenance on her face.

This wasn't like before when we would talk about Texas being a possibility or the hope of a maybe, no … She was there with us, and as she saw all the confirmations that the Lord gave us, she knew the magnitude of the moment. We were responding to it. I think all of us, including Rebekah and I, did not anticipate that after the trip we went on, we would be moving any time quickly after we got back. We would say well, maybe in one year or two years, but we also knew that the Lord could do anything on His timeline. "One day is with the Lord as a thousand years, and a thousand years as one day." (2 Peter 3:8)

After that day, it felt like a marking moment in our journey. I can humbly say that if I were to highlight a part in this story where things shifted, I would pop the cap off and highlight it right here. I feel like it was the trigger point for the windows of heaven to open over us. I felt the Lord's pleasure over us. My wife was on to something, and it was an honor to step into line with her leadership to steward this prophetic act of faith. Everything started to change from then on out. I felt like something had shifted in the spiritual realm, which was now getting ready to give birth in the natural. I can imagine it as if the Lord was peeking down on us from heaven, watching us continually go up and down the stairs with our boxes, saying to his angels, "Look how much faith they have for what I'm about to do in them. They're showing me their Faith, and I am pleased with it." As He taps them on the shoulder to peek down and see, I can't help but let my imagination take me there. The spirit air of expectation was now ever more pregnant with anticipation for what was next. We were now ready, both with boxes of our stuff and boxes of our faith. This is now the part where we were about to dig deep and grab hold of what He had for us all along, but not first without letting go.

It's a simple concept of mind; a hand must be open to receive a gift, but how can it be open if you are clinging to something so tightly? You never sit on the ground on Christmas morning and hold out your arms with your hands clinched as firm as a fist as your parents try to pass you your gifts. No, instead, you put what you had down, reach out, and get ready to receive what's coming with open hands. As your fingers extend and your palms fully expand, your hands rest under the gift, ready to catch it. The same goes if you already have something in your hand and someone is trying to give you something new. You first have to put down what you have and make room for the next gift. If you don't, you either fumble the gift you are already holding or you risk breaking the other you're reaching to grab by not having the capacity to do so. It's simple human anatomy, which is also the same as spiritual anatomy. Your hands must be rid of what's in them so you can reach out and grab what's coming to you. Many of you reading now,

I believe, are having sudden epiphanies and spontaneous thoughts rush into your mind at this very moment.

You're recounting and recalling the moments in your life that you know you were, or currently still are, holding on to something way too tightly. The Lord has asked you a long time ago to let go of these things, and there is no better time to start than right now. Is it a relationship, the refuge of your bank account, or the fortress you've created out of your comfort zone? He's asking you to let go of this for two reasons. One reason is perhaps all of your security rests in this one place. The other is He wants to know if you really actually are able to trust Him! For some, it may very well be both of those. More often than not, they are connected. He has something far better for you; I can guarantee it. It's not that He doesn't want you to have nice things. It's just that He doesn't want nice things to have you. It's not that He doesn't want you in relationships, but He doesn't want relationships to have you. How do I know that? Well, I would just say it takes one to know one. For me, the symbolic Christmas gift that I couldn't just let go of and make room for the other was my lucrative and comfortable career. Lord, help me.

I knew that I would have to face this moment at some point. I kind of put it off in my mind, hidden deep in a fortified vault, something I'd have to acknowledge at some point, but that was only if the Lord opened doors for us to move. As we know, he was flinging doors off their hinges and putting his signature on everything we were praying for. The time was approaching when the rubber was meeting the road, and a decision had to be made. Was my faith really there to trust Him with this, or was it just talk? From one tug of war to the next in this riveting adventure, I found myself at the end of this rope only with one option … surrender. Where all of my self-security, self-preservation, fortress of comfort, and refuge of finances had to come down. Surrendering it to Him was how I won. Surrendering to Him in your life is how you win. As for me and many of you reading, that is a principle that is very hard to come to grips with.

> **Surrendering to Him in your life is how you win.**

Our human minds often do not let us venture into this place of radical surrender and laid-down obedience. For many people, this is a very irrational idea because they can't imagine letting go of a beautiful 401k and a smokin' benefits package. It would be foolishness to let go of a once-in-a-lifetime opportunity that yielded more than 6-figures of a comfy checkbook and a guaranteed future RV sunset. Some people may even venture to say that this would be a decision completely void of wisdom. This is where the ways of the world and the ways of the Lord disconnect and stand at a dichotomy. The stark contrast looks like this … The world asks for a king on a throne, and Jesus comes as a baby in a manger. The world screams that go get revenge against your enemy, while the Lord says to love your enemies and pray for those who persecute you (Matthew 5:44). The culture says, "Do what makes you feel good," while Jesus says, "Deny yourself, take up your cross, and follow Me." The world says, "Follow your heart," Jesus says, "The heart is the most deceitful of all things, and is desperately wicked (Jeremiah 17: 9-10) The world says stack up all the money you can, while Jesus tips the scales and says, "Store up for yourselves treasures in heaven, where moths and vermin do not destroy (Matthew 6:19-21)." The laws of culture say, "I'll never forgive that person." Instead, the Lord says forgiveness is not an option, "If you do not forgive others their sins, your Father will not forgive your sins (Matthew 6:15)." You get the point. Cosmic differences are where one yields an earthly reward, and the other guarantees a kingdom blessing. One yields instant gratification that is promised to fade here on earth, while the other demands daily surrender, promising future glory in heaven. So, what should I do? Hold on tightly to my castle of self-security, or surrender to where I know the Lord is so terrifyingly yet so faithfully leading us? All I know is that the Lord would never lead me to a place I couldn't endure. The latter was the only viable option to choose.

Coming out of a season and the whirlwind of a year where everyone around the world, myself included, lost everything, it was only human for me to want to hold on to the one thing that seemed constant in this place of my life. My career. Week to week, paycheck to paycheck, it was o so comfortably predictable. The time was nearing, and a decision needed to be made.

Around this time in our life, after our trip, Rebekah knew we needed to set a date for when we would move. No longer a matter of "if" now but when! We were emboldened in our courage. This was something Rebekah had felt in her spirit that we were to do. She said, "If we don't set a date to do this, we will never go." She may have been right. We prayed about it and asked the Lord, "What date do you want us to move and leave here?" We couldn't explain it, but we both felt like April 1st, 2021, was the pin-point date we knew this needed to happen. No, this wasn't April Fools. We agreed and started joyfully yet sorrowfully communicating this date to our families. The more we communicated it out of our mouths, the more solidified it all seemed to get. Every time we broke the news, you could see the surprises on the faces of our family, in complete disbelief at how soon it was. "How could it be?" This was a common response among our loved ones. Some had it on their radar; to others, it was completely out of left field for them. The baffling idea to many was the "why" in the mindset of us moving. For us, no rational answer could suffice, something only crazy faith could decipher.

> **We were just riding the wave of obedience.**

We weren't "escaping away" from something and weren't

"going for" anything; we were just riding the wave of obedience.

When I look back, Abraham didn't know where he was going. All the Lord told Him was to get up "and go to a land that I will show you (Genesis 12:1)." At many stakes, this is the only verse I could fall back on to make sense of how we were both feeling. We were going to a place that he was "showing" us. For us, this was Texas. To their credit, it was true. It was soon, both for them and for us! It surely was a lot quicker and accelerated than how we initially thought it would take. We thought it was bold to think that one year or even two years was a possibility too soon. God was week by week empowering us to make decisions we both knew we never could in our own strength. The only way to describe it is as if there was a supernatural grace in this period of time to make faith-taking decisions. He was pouring out a greater measure of faith and grace for the race. The cat was out of the bag, the Gallaghers were moving, and the winds of change were swiftly blowing. There was no greater time than now to grow my wings and mount up on wings like eagles, trusting the winds of His presence and breakthrough would carry us. There still remained intimidating dominos that had to fall down. The only way they'd fall is if I would finally let the last one come down.

On this specific morning at the ungodly hour of 4 A.M., I was in full commute mode as I was well on my way to work. Recalling how I felt that day, I could feel the pressure of everything caving in around me from all the decisions we had just made and the ones yet to be. I remember, on this specific morning, spending my whole entire ride to work inquiring of the Lord. I relentlessly offered my prayers, tears, and frustrations to the Lord on this morning's drive more than I ever had before. Toiling with the decision we had made, questioning all that has led us to this point, and asking myself, "Did He really tell me to go?" Despite all the Lord has already confirmed, I settled deep into my humanistic ways and felt like I was crumbling under the weight of it all. I knew this was the week I needed to put my two-week notice in and fully show the Lord that I was going to trust Him with **all** of my future. Even when we don't want to admit it, He knows the things that we hold onto so desperately. From worshiping to praying and crying out to Him repeatedly, I brought myself to ask the Lord for another sign. "Lord, confirm this to me one last time, please, Lord. I need your assurance that this is the way, and you are here in this decision," I prayed to him desperately. As I leaned back in my seat, trying to catch my breath from my ugly crying prayer, I felt the Holy Spirit prompt me to look up. "Look up and see," I felt the Holy Spirit speak to me in my driver's seat. I picked my weary head up and saw it. Standing tall, completely illuminated as if it was the only light shining in the morning darkness, big and wide right in front of my face, "GROW YOUR WINGS" displayed in big-bold, lettered words on this billboard! "Grow Your

Wings" took up the entire billboard, with none other than an Eagle standing at the top of the illustration.

Literally, seconds after I asked the Lord for a sign, He gave me one! A sign; well, a billboard, per se. The Lord has a sense of humor. I could do nothing else but instantly weep. The presence of the Holy Spirit rushed into my car and filled the whole vehicle. I was crying, and weeping, and crying and weeping in utter disbelief. He then spoke to me again, saying, "It's time to grow your wings, son. Jump off the billboard and watch Me grow your wings on the way down." The inspiration for the title of this book, the God dream I had as a kid, the Isaiah 40:31 verse of my life, all of it had now come together in this unbelievable tapestry of faith. The billboard stared at me again as I lifted my head to see it again, and again, all I could do was weep.

The timing of the Lord was not a second too early nor a second too late; this was perfect timing. This is one of those moments where only you could know what it was like in this moment. I could venture to explain it a million times over to someone else, but it wouldn't make sense to them, and that frankly didn't matter. Only I could understand the magnitude. It was a had-to-be-there encounter with the Lord. It wasn't the billboard that caused me to weep; it was the sturdy voice of the Lord that faithfully spoke to me by telling me to "look up." It gave me all that I needed to hear. Not a recommendation, not a question, not an offer. No, this was a shout in my spirit, as if the Lord was speaking directly to me. I had never seen this billboard in my entire life, not once in the year I drove down this road. I could no longer deny that I knew that this was a fat YES to take the leap and fully trust my God. This had to be done! The phrase "grow your wings" rang in my spirit from this day on and became branded upon my heart. I was hit with another dose of fresh faith for the season! It was GO time.

That same week, I quickly drafted my two-week notice. I still have it to this day, as well as the letters of recommendation I had sought out. As I mentioned in previous chapters, God had given me tremendous favor with this company. They had taken care of me, I had done trainings for them in my prior line of work even before I worked for them, and the Lord had his hand upon me in the workplace. I prayed for several different people and saw many healings and sweet encounters with all kinds of people. Although I knew I needed to formally announce my departure from the company, before I did that, I wanted to see if there was any position in the company that would still allow me to work for them. I didn't care what it was. Put me in any department, and I'll do it. It was my thought process! I was saddened on the day I turned in my two-week notice; nonetheless, I knew it had to be done. It was one of those moments where one hand of mine reached out to hand the letter to my manager while my head looked the other way because I was sad to have to do this. The organization and leadership were totally caught off guard, even more so by a lack of understanding of why I was doing this. They would ask why I was leaving, and in my mind, I knew that there was no way they would be able to understand the complexity of what my wife and I were doing with moving our entire lives.

God was doing all of this, and let's face it, not everyone is going to be able to understand that. This was not my own will or strength; this was Him. "My wife and I are moving to Texas", I would say, and subsequently, they would raise their eyebrows as high as they would go as if communicating to me, "Dude, you're completely out of your mind." My desperate attempts to try and get people to understand what God was doing in our lives never worked. The more I tried to make people understand, the more disappointed I would sometimes be. The enemy often would try and play on this and attack my mind. "Look Jake, it doesn't even make sense to anyone. I told you that you were crazy. This was never going to work, and I tried to tell you, Texas has nothing for you, you're going to lose everything." Those were the kind of thoughts that would race in my head as I faltered in my ability to make people understand. Those thoughts were not going to win, for I trusted the Lord with this.

Two-week notice was handed in, and in the unfortunate response of the company's top leadership, there was going to be no position available for me to step into outside of the one I already had. I had a slight hope that there would be something for me, but that wind had now quickly been taken out of my sail. Exhaling in sadness at that news, the reality of this whole journey now had become ever so real; trusting him with a job was going to be fully in His hands. It then all became evident to me that I had only about two more weeks to say goodbye to all the people on the job site and the people I had developed relationships with. It saddened me. I had a strong rapport with just about everybody in my workplace and was dreading having to say goodbye to that. Day by day continued to pass by as my two-week work notice began to dwindle.

I got to the point where I had one week of work left to complete, and then this happened. The same individual who had communicated to me that there was no opportunity available for me in the company then contacted me again. On February 6th, 2021, at 1:06 PM, he called me, and I missed his call, but he left a voicemail. He wanted to talk to me about something. I got off work that day and then got the chance to ring him back while I was on the road home. He told me that something had been on his mind for some time, and he had to do something about it. He said, "I've been losing sleep over losing you here at the company, and I couldn't help but make a few calls on your behalf. I talked to the corporate department, and I know a guy who works in Corporate who has been trying to hire someone on his team for some time now," he communicated this to me as my heart started to shake in anticipation. "The only catch is that it may be a pretty big pay cut from where you are now. However, he wants to talk to you. Give him a call tomorrow at 4 PM on Monday. I couldn't let myself lose a guy like you in the company." My whole body was shaking as I hung up the phone call in utter disbelief at what had just happened.

Even though I had not received the job yet, I knew it was well on its way! This was a miracle! The Lord was working behind the scenes even when I couldn't see it. The Lord gave me a favor and moved upon the heart of my bosses boss to make way for me. I relayed the news to my wife as soon as I could dial her number, and her reaction was the same as mine; utter disbelief filled with tears. I told my family just as much, and they cried in celebration of God's goodness. "This is God", they all said. God was rewarding our faithfulness to trust him, and finally, seeing this evidence changed the game.

I contacted the Corporate leader at the appointed time, but he did not answer. The suspense was killing me! "I need to have this call, and I need to have it now," I thought to myself as I waited with excruciating eagerness. He told me he had received my call but was very busy and re-scheduled It for the next day. The next day came quicker than the blink of an eye, and there I was, in the park, pacing back and forth, sweating and shaking while hearing the phone dial ring in my ear as I called him once more. He answered! He was super easygoing as our small talk ensued. He then quickly cut to the chase. "This position I'm about to offer you wasn't even going to be available until 2022. However, I've been constantly hearing amazing things about you.

From managers on the job site to project leaders, and funny enough, even my dad has said amazing things about you." "Your dad?" I replied. He name-dropped his name to me, and it dawned on me that the 3rd party contractor I met with weekly on my job site to go over site management and compliance was actually his dad! "What in the world?" I thought to myself. He continued, "My dad has spoken so highly of you, and from the look of the numbers on our records, you have also had the highest amount of problems found and problems solved on your job site. Congratulations." He continued to honor me and celebrate me throughout the conversation to then lead right into what was on the other side. He told me, "Given the success and reputation of your production, I want to accelerate this job opening for you. 2022 was going to be the year when this position became available. However, I'm going to accelerate this opening just for you. I formally want to offer you a position to work with the Corporate team, my team, for I know you will be an asset. I also ran the numbers and compared your current salary to what I can offer you, and it will be quite a pay cut". I thought to myself, "Well, what kind of number does quite a pay cut mean?" As if he heard my thoughts, he quickly spoke again and said, "After the numbers, your pay would be two dollars less an hour than what you are getting now." "This guy has to be kidding me," I thought to myself as tears flowed down my eyes. "Is that something that can work for you?" he asked. I cleared my throat and said, "Yeah, I think I can work with that," acting as if this number was such a compromise for me, knowing it was a huge blessing.

I accepted the job offer immediately after our conversation, but this isn't even where the miracles stop. Given Rebekah and I had already set a date for our departure, we really desired to take a month off before we left and dedicate our time to spend with our families. We wanted to savor a month with all of them before we left. I brought this up to my now-new boss and nervously asked him, "Would it be okay if I took the month of March off to spend with my family before our big move and then start work first thing when we get to Texas?" He acted like this was a walk in the park: "Of course you can do that. I'll start filing your transfer papers now, and you can also work another week on your current job if that helps supplement some income for you during that time!" "Are you sure?" I replied. "Of course, whatever you need," he responded. From the miraculous offer of a job right up my alley to every hurdle I thought about that could be a problem, it was all light-leg work to my Father in Heaven. Throughout these series of events, the Lord's hand being mightily faithful in my life was evident. As I gave Him the last thing I was holding on to, He gave me more in return than I could have imagined. My trust was fully His, and He rewarded us through it. He has been a Gentleman while he opened the doors no man could shut, and a Protector while closing the doors that no man could open. Isaiah 22:22 was live in real time for us now. He wasn't just "opening" the doors for us;

He was "building" them and then flinging them wide! Positions that weren't supposed to be available, He forced time to yield to His hand. "It's time to grow your wings, son. Jump off the billboard and watch Me grow your wings on the way down." That was what He spoke to me on that morning drive, already knowing what He had waiting for me on the other side. It was happening; I was now growing my wings on the way down, and now my wife and I were stepping into grace for the race.

10

Grace for the Race

"Come to me, all who labor and heavy laden, and I will give you rest. Take My yoke upon you, and learn from me, for I am gentle and lowly in heart, and you will find rest for your souls. For my yoke is **easy**, and My burden is light." (Matthew 11:28-30) In bold red letters, this scripture lends us an invitation to step in. Jesus Himself is speaking to us. For the young or old, rich or poor, strong or weak, near or far, no one is more worthy to receive this from Him than you are right now. Take the yoke of this world off you and receive His yoke today; the yoke that is **easy**. That's exactly what everything began to feel like as we stepped into His grace for the race. Easy.

The dam broke, and the river of grace was now mightily rushing into every area of our lives. The Lord was running the show, and at this point, we were happy to let Him. I felt like my legs were moving, but it was Him pushing us in the back, propelling us forward into His will. It was His grace.

The mountain that stood before us had been made low, and the valley that seemed impossible to enter was raised up. After I had completely let go and let God in and, in return, received my new job, a cascade of blessings began rushing quickly behind me. The miraculous breakthrough of my new position was only a precursor to the more that was coming. Days later, Rebekah also landed a new remote position, we sold our second car in a matter of hours (the Lord led us just to leave California with one car), we pinpointed the area we were going to live in with prayer, we found an apartment that approved us and paid our down deposit, and even to my wife's delight, we got her dream; a baby golden retriever just to add to the fun (we had no clue what we were in for). I couldn't even keep up with what was transpiring. At one point, I had to open up a notes section on my phone just to keep track of all that He was doing for us, as my wife urged me to remember all He was doing in us. His goodness and grace were running after us.

All the obstacles and hurdles I had in the back of my mind that hindered my faith in this move were seemingly completed in weeks. His yoke really was easy. It felt like the Lord just snapped His fingers, and boom, it was all done. Look at God! At one point, it seemed like I was just pushed off to the side, simply watching the Lord knock domino after domino down on this wild journey. It was like He moved me aside and said, "Jake, you did your part, your faith has pleased me, thank you for putting your weight on Me, now just sit back and watch Me do what I do." Once the breakthrough was flowing, it was flowing hard. From chapter 3, where I felt like all I was hitting was "brass heavens," I now felt the direct opposite. We were hitting the "bullseye of heaven," striking the mark with the arrows of our faith. The Lord knew we would need great faith for this season, so in that, he gave us great grace. We had jumped off the billboard, put our weight on Him, trusted Him, and felt like we were now catching the wind of His empowering presence.

I don't know if you have ever felt in life like the very thing standing before you was seemingly impossible to overcome or conquer. I know I have. A mountain that was standing in front of you, or a valley that stooped below you, or maybe a wall that seemed impossible to scale. It all seemed humanly impossible … until Him. There's one thing to have faith in: God can do something, and it's an entirely different thing to trust in Him. Faith is the belief system. Trust is the actionable evidence of your belief system. If you are looking at a chair in front of you that you're getting ready to sit on, you look at it and have the "belief system" (faith) that that chair can hold you. It was designed to do what it does, tested, manufactured for its purpose, and predicted that it would carry out its ability. You believe the chair has the capacity to withhold your weight. You believe it was designed to keep you up. Trust is when you actually take your "belief system" and finally put your weight on it. You sit down on the chair, you put your weight on what you believed in, and now your faith has evidence to be seen.

God is waiting for people to take the trust they've placed in themselves and put their weight on Him instead. Faith says, "I know you are God Almighty in my life, and You are good towards me," but trust says, "I will make you Lord of my decisions and show you my obedience even when my faith can't see." People who fully **trust** in the Lord sound like this: "I don't know what it's going to look like, but I'm going to do it anyway because You said to. I don't know where this road leads to, but I fully trust you because You're the One who gave me the address. I don't understand what You're doing this season, but you told me to "GO," so I'm going pack up my stuff and go. I have no clue how this small business of mine is going to prosper, but I'm going to launch it anyway because You said the time is now. I don't know how to start a podcast, but I'm going to buy the microphone anyway because You said so. I've never stepped foot on a track, but here goes nothing because I know You told me to run that marathon. I don't know how to write a book, but you told me to do it, so here I am, just trying to put one word in front of the other (that one was for me)." In whatever example you may connect with, I have something to say to you: it's time to trust in Him and grow your wings. Many of you reading may be laughing right now because if the Lord asked you to run a marathon, you'd say that wasn't from God. Only speaking from personal experience! Every one of those statements shifts all the responsibility onto God rather than putting the trust in ourselves alone. You may be asking yourself, why does that matter? Well, the real and raw truth is that there are going to be things in life that God will ask us to do that are well beyond our own human ability. In this, He gets the glory, lest any of us should boast. Let us not abort the dreams and callings He has on our lives because our measuring stick stops at us. This is what His grace is for. It gives us the supernatural ability to accomplish far beyond what our natural selves ever could. To dream the unthinkable, to reach the unreachable, and touch the untouchable. When your faith and trust collide, and you make Him the Lord of your life, He then gives you grace for the race. I believe some of you reading this right now are actually going to be feeling a fresh breath of life breathed into you and your spirit. For some, it is a second wind. Pray this prayer with me, "Lord, I pray that your Holy Spirit and fresh breath of life would fill me once again. I pray this in Jesus' name." Every reader who has their eyes on this page right now has a fresh breath to breathe again, a fresh breath to dream again, and a fresh breath to dust off those passions and desires He placed in us, which are within reach. It's been decided.

It's time to grow your wings again.

11

Legacy is Born

On the other side of your obedience stands the people whose life depends on your yes. Believe it or not, you carry much more worth than you may think. Your decisions and actions speak a very loud message not only to your present time but, more importantly, to your future, which is yet to be experienced. At the end of this book, if you don't see the value and worth that you behold alongside the beautiful passions and desires that are inside of you, just know as I type this, I am at the same time praying that you will see it once again or begin to see it for the first time. There is an immeasurable amount of value within you that was strategically placed there to come alive at this specific point in time. Not just for you but for the sake of the world and others. I remember that, as a kid in grade school (I don't remember the exact grade), the teacher was teaching about sound waves. I am not too sure if it was an absolute fact or truth that was stated. However, it has stuck with me throughout the decades because it speaks to me. She told the class, "Did you know that when you speak your words out, and someone hears you, they are hearing the sound waves created by your voice? Your ears, for a point in time, are able to catch the sound waves and hear the sound that someone else's vocal cords created. After they hear the sound of your voice for that split second enter their ears, their attention is caught. Have you ever asked yourself where those sound waves go? Do they just disappear and go away forever, do they go in one ear and right out the next, do they die off and fall to the ground, or do your soundwaves continue to go throughout all of the earth? Your words never stop moving, and they actually travel all around the world again and again. So, be careful what you say. Speak life with your mouth, for what you say will never go away." Even if one future generation cannot hear the voice of the past one, it does not mean the words of the former are still not speaking to us and moving throughout the earth. I believe one "yes" can echo into a generation and transform your children's children. That's what I believe this story about growing my wings is even about. It's not even about me. It is about the legacy to come after. It's about growing your wings now so they can soar on His wings later. I am simply a piece and a vessel being moved to bring forth the more God has in store. It is bigger than you thought, I guarantee you.

As mentioned in earlier chapters, God spoke to Abram, who later became "Father Abraham," to get up and leave his father's house. He was a piece that God moved so the Lord could bring forth the seed of promise and the seed of blessing in time to come—generations after him. Abraham did not see everything with his own two eyes, nor did he know what was to come in times after, but even so, in his obedience, he allowed his yes to echo into the generations. The sound waves of his voice and obedience never fell to the ground. Romans 4:19, in the word of God, even says that Abraham "was as good as dead," yet the Lord still took him and used him to "become the father of many nations." Think of that to yourself right now for a moment. The Lord took for himself a man who was as good as nothing, lifeless, no future present in his own ability, and yet made him the "father of faith"! Maybe this is you right now in this season of your life, and you feel as though you are "as good as nothing," "worthless," or even depressed enough to say, "as good as dead." Believe it or not, you're in the absolute perfect position for the Lord to transform and change the world through you. You're the perfect candidate for His glory. This is what the story of Grow Your Wings is all about. Where the Lord takes a boy whose father was told that he would never be able to have him and show His glory! He takes a story with a clear end in sight according to the world, but the Lord intervenes because He still has more to say. The Lord says to that boy who is now a man, "You are a miracle child, and I will give you miracle children." He is faithful.

As miracle after miracle and open door after open door continued to fling wide open for Rebekah and me on this wild journey of ours, I heard the Lord speak to me, "You better be writing all of this down. This will be a book one day." So, why write this book other than the reasons I alluded to at the beginning of this story? Well, it's simple. Just to be obedient to what He said. Hear God and obey God. You'd be surprised to see what takes place when you do. For all the readers reading this, my children, my family, my friends, and whoever may come across this autobiography, it is time to grow your wings. The earth is crying out for your faith and obedience to change history and move within the earth. There is something in you that you carry that no one else could release into this earth quite like you can. It's time to do it. Growing your wings takes courage. Courage does not deny that you fear the giant standing before you. Courage is knowing that even though there is, and you feel afraid, that giant does not get to author how your story ends. There's already someone who wrote that story, and His name is Christ, the Lord of hosts. Let His courage become your courage today as you lean into Him and let Christ claim your victory. As my final sentence in this faith-

> **The earth is crying out for your faith and obedience to change history.**

taking adventure of a biography, I'd like to leave you with this—"Grow your wings and dedicate your life to risk-taking faith, for **your greatest place of warfare shall become your greatest place of inheritance.**"

Made in the USA
Columbia, SC
22 April 2025